FUTURE ENTERPRISE

QUANTUM COMPUTING & ARTIFICIAL INTELLIGENCE

Future Enterprise

Second Edition – March 2022

info@quantumy.ai

UAE National Media Council approval no. **MC-01-01-6292411**

Age Classification: E

"The age group that suits the content of the books has been classified and determined according to the age classification system issued by the National Media Council"

ISBN: **978-9948-19-201-5**

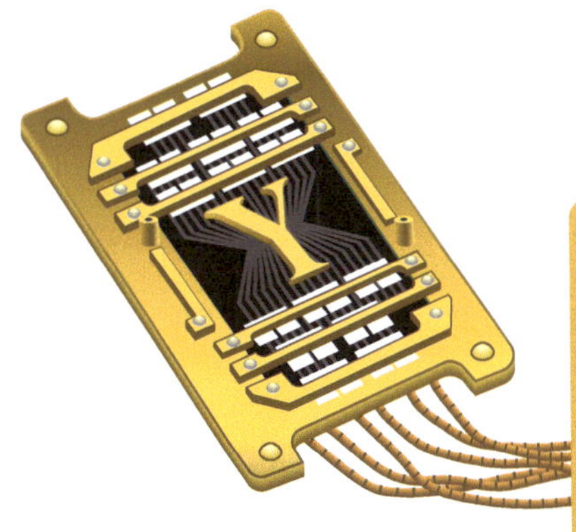

To Mustafa

Despite how short you experienced life on Earth, what we saw in your life was the embodiment of strength.

The strength in our memories with you endlessly feeds our souls no matter how much time has passed.

They are what made this book and many other things that we never thought were possible, a reality.

Table of Contents

Introduction

Looking ahead and planning are the right paths to pioneer, become effective, and take the initiative. In this era, nothing will discourage nations from seeking to own new technology. In our public and private institutions, technology is still so ambiguous, whether for the general staff or for decision-makers who are not technological specialists. This can lead to wasting the organization's resources in digital transformation projects due to a blurring of vision and impossible promises of technology companies. In this book, we set a general framework for digital transformation projects. We also try to make Artificial Intelligence and quantum computing, which are truly technologies of the future, comprehensible so that employees in public and private organizations can understand this technology and adapt it to turn their institutions into «smart» organizations.

This book combines the experience of the elderly and modernity of youth, as it is composed by two authors from different generations. This book combines both practical experiences and academic approaches in order to target the future. Our goal was, and is still, to simplify information technology and communicate it to different readers in their respective language. We hope that we might help in the renaissance of our Arab countries, preserve their resources, and increase their productivity.

This book has combined three main topics: digital transformation, Artificial Intelligence, and quantum computing. This book combines these topics together without complicated technical terminologies that would alienate the non-specialist reader. Furthermore, this book combines scientific theories, historical information, scientific news, scientific experiments, and even financial reports to appeal to a diversity of minds. Accordingly, all information aims to seamlessly reach each reader's mind and sentiment.

The project still has other hopes and greater ambitions. We may yet reach them with the grace of God and support of our dear reader.

Dubai, United Arab Emirates,

25 Jumada I 1442, corresponding to 9 January 2021

CHAPTER 1

FROM A-JAZARI TO ELON MUSK

1.1 Wisdom is the lost property of people

Since the beginning of creation, people have sought to fulfill their duties and achieve their goals with the least amount of effort in the shortest period of time. The less effort exerted and the greater goal accomplished, the more this is considered a great success by the people.

People used to have children to help them overcome the physical hardships and security concerns of life. They were either a hand that helped them in their work or a sword that terrorized or struck their enemies, whether human or non-human. There were times where people enslaved other people. Other times, they made tools and machines or invaded other societies to obtain their human, material and natural resources. In all of these activities, they were pursuing their goals, regardless of whether they were right or wrong.

In all such cases and attempts, people were trying to achieve their goals in the most efficient way by saving effort, time, and resources. What distinguishes humans from other creatures is that humans learn from their attempts and seek to avoid repeating their mistakes. Most importantly, they transmit those experiences - whether they were successful or not- to other humans. These experiences then accumulate to form «wisdom.» It was said that, «Wisdom is the lost property of the believer, so wherever he finds it, he has a better right to it.» It is a treasure that only few have acquired, and even fewer who have been able to make the best use of it.

1.1 Wisdom is the lost property of people

Scientists have tried to classify the stages that people go through in order to reach their desired goal of wisdom. Despite their disagreements about what they called the knowledge pyramid and its variations, it is still one of the ideal forms to describe maturity stages of our perception of our surroundings, or, in other words, to describe how human knowledge develops.

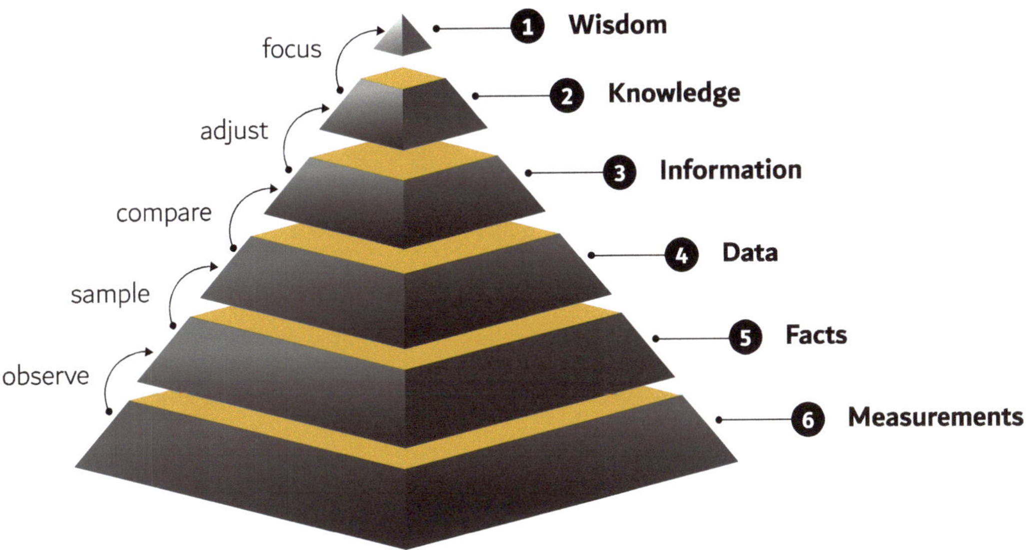

Figure 1.1: Knowledge Pyramid: some definitions start only from the data level and above. Data is nothing but the facts which we have recorded and measured from the surrounding environment.

Data is a record of facts measured from the surrounding environment, it is just a set of symbols or numbers, such as temperatures or heights of a group of people. Data itself is useless, just as any other raw material that was extracted from nature and not processed.

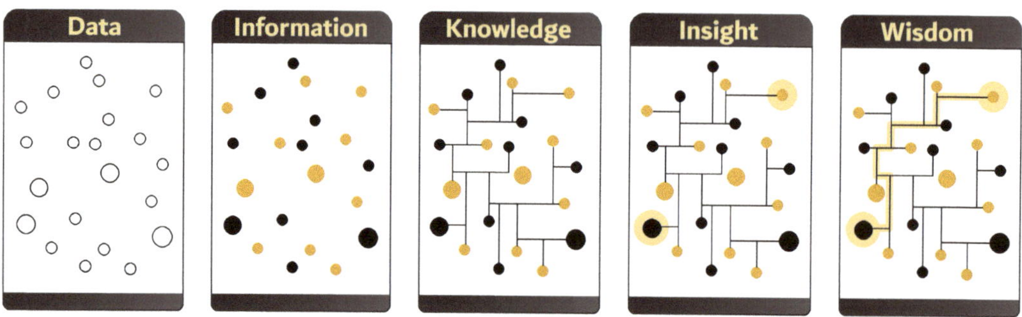

Figure 1.2: Knowledge Pyramid from another - perhaps clearer - angle showing another stage of development, «insight.» We will see another diagram of this Knowledge Pyramid later when talking about Big Data.

Data needs a context (or a specific domain of **knowledge**) on the basis of which it can be organized and classified to become meaningful information with which questions such as «what», «when,» and «who» can be answered. This «meaning» may or may not be useful.

Then, we reach the most important step in our journey, knowledge. This is the product of our ability to learn from accumulated information, whether through time or different experiences which we have gone through simultaneously. If we are able to refine it and extract its prevailing patterns, then we have the «knowledge» necessary to understand the context of this information. It becomes our tool to perceive the facts that lie within the information and data.

When «knowledge» matures and our insight to discern the facts becomes clearer and stronger, we can extract the basic principles, rules, and notions in every context and field that we are trying to understand and study. This is the wisdom that we seek, and by which we can build models to anticipate and predict the future from the data that we collect.

Artificial Intelligence is just our attempt to extract «wisdom» and put it in a form or a **model** that a «machine» can use to deduce results from the data that we provide it with. It is the most advanced technology that society has currently reached. With people having invented machines to do physical labor, they now want computers to replace the entire human mind.

1.2 Father of Robotics: Ismail Al-Jazari

Being aware of the origin and history of something is a way to understand and appreciate its importance. We must mention in this chapter the father of robotics, the Arab Muslim scholar Badi' Al-Zaman Abu Al-Izz ibn Ismail ibn Al-Razzaz Al-Jazari (1136- 1206 AD), nicknamed «Al-Jazari.» Al-Jazari lived and excelled in the Diyarbakir region on the borders between Iraq and Turkey.

The engineering ideas and solutions developed by Al-Jazari in his most famous book, «The Book of Knowledge of Ingenious Mechanical Devices,» are still the basis for many mechanical machines today. Al-Jazari's knowledge provided one of the foundations of the scientific renaissance in the Arab-Islamic civilization, which was later transferred to Europe.

Figure 1.3: The «castle clock» is another invention of Al-Jazari. It was a 3.4 meter multi-functional complex device. Besides timekeeping, it displayed the zodiac and solar and lunar orbits. One of its tools was a pointer in the shape of the crescent moon which travelled across the top of the clock gateway, moved by a hidden cart, and caused automatic doors to open, each revealing a mannequin every hour. The castle clock also had five automata musicians who automatically play music when moved by levers operated by a hidden camshaft attached to a water wheel.

The American historian, Lynn White, and many Western scholars have admitted that several designs of machines invented by Al-Jazari were transferred to Europe. They have stated that Segmental gears clearly first appear in Al-Jazari's books, while in the West they emerge in Giovanni de Dondi's astronomical clock two centuries after Al-Jazari. Al-Jazari was also the first to talk about the crankshaft, invented water-raising machines, and used metal balls to indicate time in water clocks. Indeed, one evidence of his greatness is that when he invented the hydro-power-driven water supply machine, he left a place for an animal that appeared to drag the machine crankshaft so as not to terrify people into thinking that the machine was powered with magic!

Al-Jazari even built a robot in the form of a boy pouring water and then providing a towel, a comb, and a mirror after ablution. With his passion for music, he also built a musical automaton, a boat with four automatic musicians that floated on a lake to entertain guests at royal drinking parties.

1.3 What Is Intelligence?

The simplest things that you do in your life may seem very complicated if you want to divide them into a series of even simpler tasks. For example, when you drive your car to work, you may think that it is a simple task, and even your mind may mostly focus on other things. However, it is not as simple as that. In addition to your driving skills, you memorize the road, understand the meanings of its signs, consistently check the placement of the cars around you, estimate their speeds and maintain a safe distance, and even try to understand other drivers' intentions, either from their signals or their way of driving, as well as pedestrians' intentions when they are trying to cross the road—sometimes not even at a pedestrian crosswalk.

That is not all! You must initially know what the road is, for it may be an asphalt road bordered by two barriers, two sidewalks, or nothing at all. Through large intersections, you must find your own way from your direction to the perpendicular direction, even though it is a road with no marked lanes.

Perhaps you are now well aware that driving a car, even for those of you considered unskilled drivers, is a matter that needs intelligence, and in order for us to create a «smart machine», it was necessary for scientists to first analyze «intelligence» into its primary components:

1.3.1 Perception

People perceive the world around them through their five senses, chiefly through hearing and sight. In other creatures, perception abilities may differ. Some organisms may use ultrasound, such as bats, while others may use heat receptors. Referring to the above example of driving a car, automated driving systems use a combination of «perceptual devices», such as cameras, motion sensors, etc. These sensors help the automated driving system perceive the car's surroundings including people, other cars, and any inanimate objects such as trees and poles.

1.3.2 Reasoning

Reasoning is related to the human ability to think and find relationships between things, especially causalities. It is also what makes a person able to solve problems, or what is called «Problem Solving.»

1.3.3 Planning

When you drive your car and determine your destination in advance, you involuntarily translate that destination or «goal» into a set of tasks related to driving the car. Additionally, you may review Google Maps to ensure you take the best and fastest route or try to remember the best places to park your car. Whatever you do to prepare to attain this «goal» is what we call planning.

1.3.4 Knowledge Representation

We can consider the different senses and methods of perception as tools for collecting data and information. Then, we use thinking and logic to rearrange and analyze the data and information to form knowledge. We have to ask here: How do we preserve knowledge, rather than data? If I give you a list of things (for example: mountain- flag - ocean - lion), mention the word «wind,» and ask you to name the things cited in the list that remind you of the wind, you will most likely point out (flag - ocean). Furthermore, if I mention «height» then you may choose (mountain - flag), and so on.

We can understand here, in a simple way, the dilemma of knowledge preservation, or what scholars call «knowledge representation.» How can a machine preserve knowledge in the same way as humans? The problem of knowledge preservation is one of the major obstacles to developing «General Artificial Intelligence.» How can a machine, when it learns a principle such as «speed» in the car driving field, use the same principle in weather forecasting, but wind speed?

1.3.5 Language

People read, write, and speak language, which is their means of communication with others. Language is also their means to preserve and exchange knowledge. People can summarize a topic they read or divide a group of books and articles into sub-groups on different classification bases, such as topics, size, country of origin, or the author's background, and even according to a subgroup of these categories. In addition, the vocabulary of a language may be understood differently depending on the context (for example, the word «state» in a political book would be interpreted completely differently than in a physics book).

1.3.6 Social Intelligence

If a person was standing on the side of the road and moving his hand while you were driving your car, you might go on your way, change lanes, or stop to allow them to ride with you, although the hand movement might be the same in all cases. What differs in each case is your interpretation of this person's hand movement according to the appearance of the person who did it. It might be a signal to other passers-by or drivers, a warning signal because their car was broken down and stopped a few meters away along the side of the road, or the driver of the broken down car wanted you to drive them somewhere, and many other possibilities.

In all cases, you use «social intelligence» to interpret this simple movement, which is a mixture of the intelligence components mentioned above. It requires «perception» then «logic» and «knowledge» preserved from similar situations that you have experienced. Then, you make a decision to stop or not to stop based on the «planning» you did before driving your car!

When you read the comments on your post on a social network site, you might read and understand the same sentence (for example: «can you really do it?») in different ways. It might be a mockery, a real question, or even a praise or wonder about your abilities!

1.3.7 Motion and Manipulation

This section is the base field of robotics research, which means, as its name suggests, people's ability to move in their surroundings, relocate from place to place, and plan for this process. The motion task is broken down into «primitive» tasks. This motion process may be accompanied by carrying an object, displacing another object, and so on.

Scientists have found that motion is more complex than reasoning (section 1.3.2), and that teaching a computer how to play chess or any other game may be easier than teaching it the motion skills of a one-year-old child.[1]

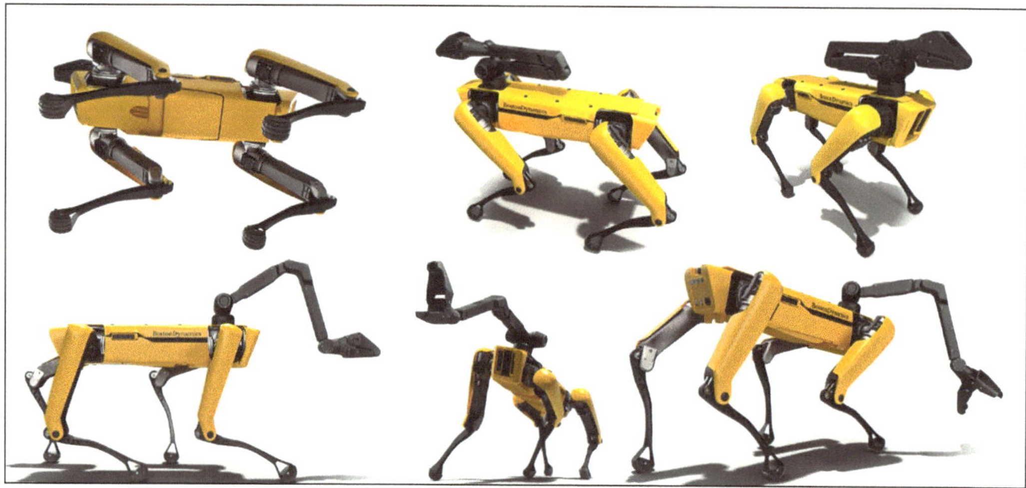

Figure 1.4: The Spot Robot from Boston Dynamics. It is already being sold to construction companies and manufactures.

However, during recent years, motion research and applications have made huge leaps, and we now have robots that can jump, run, and avoid obstacles, but most of them are still tested in corporate laboratories or displayed at technology fairs around the world.

1 Moravec's paradox

1.4 Definition of Artificial Intelligence

Artificial Intelligence has many definitions, but we will only study two of them. The first defines Artificial Intelligence as:

«a wide-ranging branch of computer science concerned with building smart machines capable of performing tasks that typically require human intelligence.»

In this definition, we understand to which scientific fields AI belongs. We recognize that it is related to machines and software. However, we still don't understand the meaning of «intelligence» in its correct context and the relationship of this intelligence with human intelligence. So, let's see the second definition:

«A machine's capability of performing tasks intelligently without being explicitly instructed.»

When you enter your destination into your car's GPS, this GPS has no previous information about your destination, and no one else has entered instructions that allows the GPS to lead you to that particular destination. However, GPS makers used an algorithm that enables the system to find the best and fastest route to reach your destination. This is what we can call «Intelligence».

In order to understand more about what Artificial Intelligence is, before addressing its details, let us see some examples[2] which many of us use, whether we know they work by Artificial Intelligence or not:

---

2 «AI for Everyone» course, Andrew Ng

Inputs	Outputs	App name
Email	Spam or not	**Spam filtering**
Audio recording	Text	**Speech recognition systems**
English text	Arabic text	**Machine translation (example: Google)**
Image and sensor information	Car placements	**Automated driving systems**
X-ray images	Text	**Diagnosis systems**

Table 1.1: Examples of Artificial Intelligence applications

Based on these examples, we can understand the general shape of Artificial Intelligence systems and applications. As shown in the above table, each application has specific inputs to be processed to produce (or predict) the desired outputs. These outputs vary; they may be a yes or no answer, as in the applications of spam filtering and text, or even coordinates, as in the case of automated car systems.

Let us address the second definition in light of these examples. We can define «spam filtering» system as an application of Artificial Intelligence as follows:

«It is the ability of the email system to filter emails and recognize spam sent by people or organizations that might have never sent messages to this email before, and the content of the spam might have never been received in any other email.»

1.5 Artificial Intelligence: The Possible and the Impossible?

Artificial Intelligence evolution can be classified into the following stages:

1. **Narrow Artificial Intelligence (NAI)**

NAI is the ability of a machine to perform one or more specific tasks that normally require human intelligence. That task is simple in one context or area, such as recognition of a person's face from among millions of other faces. Unfortunately, we have not made much progress at this stage. All we could do was build a multipartite system in which every part performs a specific task. Then, these parts are integrated together to form a multi-tasking system. The closest example to this system is the self-driving system in which several tasks are integrated to allow it to drive a car.

2. **Broad Artificial Intelligence (BAI)**

BAI is an intermediate stage between Narrow Artificial Intelligence and General Artificial Intelligence. If there was a system that was trained to perform a specific task in a specific field and could then perform another task in the same field without prior training, it would be considered one of the Broad Artificial Intelligence systems. An example of this would be a face recognition system that can differentiate between a dog and a cat image without having been trained on this task before.

3. General Artificial Intelligence (GAI)

GAI is the ability of a machine to do any task a human can do. This is a comprehensive approach that almost covers all the above-mentioned parts under the definition of intelligence. In other words, a robot would simulate humans in almost all capabilities, including moving, thinking, speaking, etc. While Elon Musk has already launched a project to build the first «General Artificial Intelligence system», Andrew Ng, an Artificial Intelligence pioneer of our time, said in one of his lectures that it is not known when this type of Artificial Intelligence can be developed.[3].

4. Super Artificial Intelligence (SAI)

SAI is the kind of Artificial Intelligence featured in science fiction novels and movies, where we see a robot that cannot be distinguished from a human. It can even surpass all human capabilities, including thinking and moving. Another example is a software that tries to control the world because its intelligence has surpassed the human intelligence.

---

3 Elon Musk is the founder of Tesla, manufacturer of electric vehicles. Andrew Ng is one of the most important researchers of Artificial Intelligence. Ng is a co-founder of an Artificial Intelligence division at Google, called «Google Brain»

Figure: 1.5: Artificial Intelligence Levels

According to the above-mentioned definitions, our study will address «Narrow Artificial Intelligence.» Here, Andrew Ng sets a simple criterion by which it can be determined whether the task that we are dealing with can be performed by Artificial Intelligence or not. This «If» criterion is that «if an **experienced** person can do a mental task with less than one second of thought, we can probably automate it using AI.» Determining the positions of the cars around you while driving does not require more than one second. The same also applies when identifying the picture of one of your acquaintances or any similar issues and tasks.

Here, we will need to explain the term «experienced» a little more. What experience do you need to determine the cars' positions around you or to identify the photo of one of your friends? Let's first take a clearer example. If you got an X-ray of someone's lungs, you would not be able to determine whether this person has pneumonia or not. Even if you looked at the X-ray for a hundred years, you would not know unless you were an experienced pulmonologist. So, let's return to the knowledge pyramid again.

The doctor's experience led him to the «wisdom» that allowed him to recognize pneumonia at a glance.

So, what experience do you need to determine the cars' positions around you? You simply need to see cars of multiple sizes and shapes. Although it is available to almost all people, it is still an acquired experience. In addition, you cannot recognize the photo of a person you have never met before, and you may even need to meet them several times during which their appearance might undergo changes (clothing, hair length, beard, etc.), and only then might you recognize this person's picture in less than one second, even if their appearance has changed due to age or some disguise (sunglasses, head cover, etc.).

As a matter of fact, the concept of «experience» for a machine is still different from that for humans. The information which forms the «experience» in the machine must match the structure of the information that the machine receives if it was asked to derive an output. For example, if you only trained the machine to recognize the side-profile portrait of a person, it may not be able to recognize this person if you provide it with his front-on portraits.

1.6 Challenges of Artificial Intelligence

During the contemporary history of Artificial Intelligence development, scientists faced challenges that hindered their way to reaching the desired goals of smart machines. We have to examine these challenges before addressing Artificial Intelligence in more details:

- **Powerful Computer (High Performance Computing)**

Computers must have powerful processors that can perform millions of mathematical and logical operations per second so that they search through the input data and find the optimal model for the problem in question, such as «weather forecasting» or «facial recognition.» These processors were not available during the previous decades. Even at the present time, the matter is still relative. The more we deal with complex issues, the stronger our computing structures and capabilities will need to be. In fact, certain Artificial Intelligence models can only be trained in large universities laboratories, while others can only be developed and trained in big companies such as Google.

- **Data Availability**

To solve a problem, scientists or «machines» must have access to sufficient data and information to «learn» from, understand the problem, and then solve it. This also was not available in previous decades. Here, too, the matter remains relative. We must provide accurate and sufficient data. Ever since the emergence of interactive websites that allow users to share and modify content, such as social platforms, the amount of data added per second exceeded the amount that was uploaded on the Internet until the launch of Facebook.

- **Artificial Intelligence Algorithms**

Like any other science, this niche needs continuous research to reach theories which contribute to its development. Artificial Intelligence is a distinguished field as it depends on algorithms[4].

When stronger algorithms emerge, the efficiency and speed of Artificial Intelligence systems improves. In addition, Artificial Intelligence algorithms are based on probability and statistics. However, a large part of algorithms was not even developed during previous decades. For example, the paradigm shift that occurred in neural network technology was a product of one or more algorithms published by a scientist to solve the problems of neural networks[5].

---

4 Algorithms are a set of mathematical and sequential logic steps necessary to solve a problem. Algorithm (in Arabic «Khwarizmiyah») was named after Abu Jaafar Muhammad ibn Musa al-Khwarizmi, who invented it in the ninth century AD.

5 In 1986, Paul Smolensky introduced the «Restricted Boltzmann Machine.» In 2006, Geoffrey Hinton and others invented fast learning algorithms that could work with these «machines.» Both inventions were considered by some a paradigm shift for neural networks.

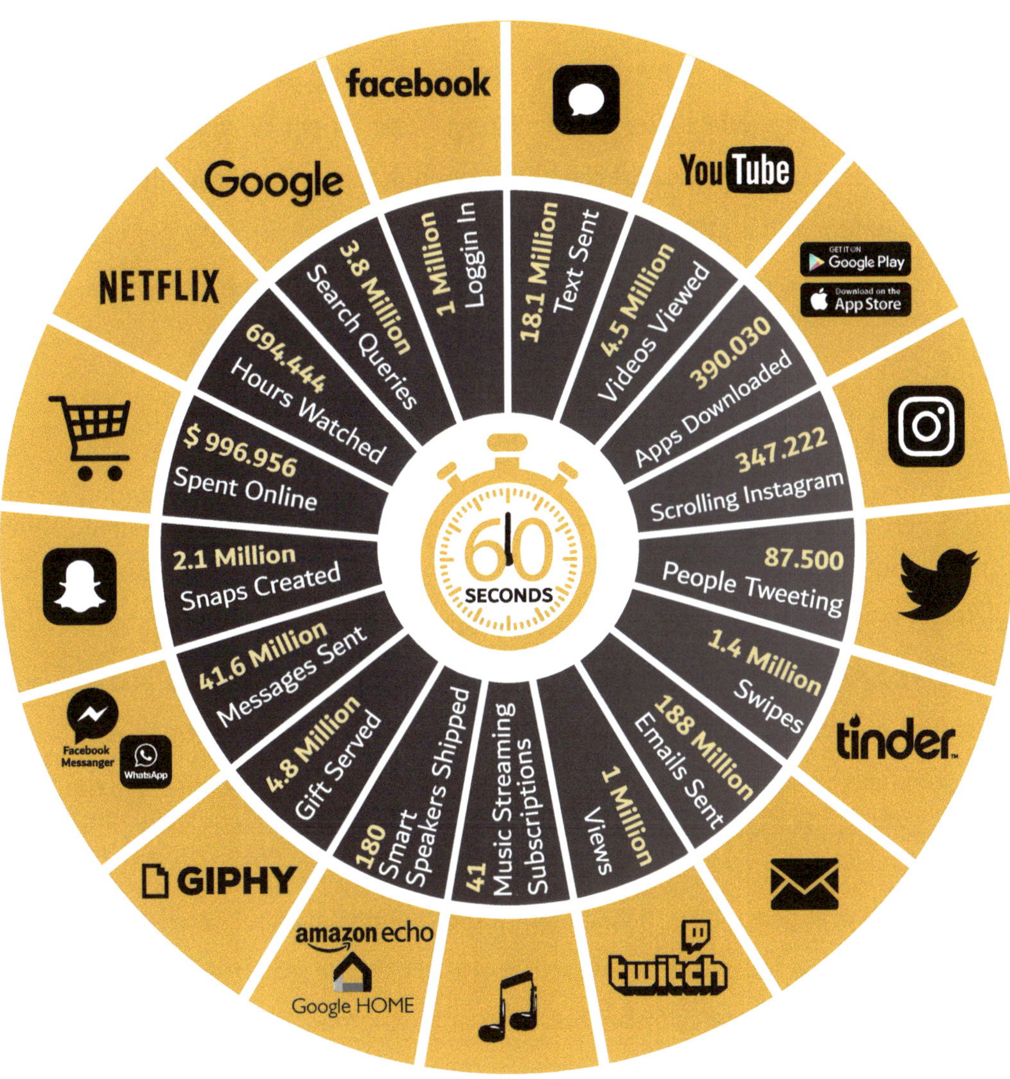

Figure 1.4: Big Data in 2019

- **Used Energy**

Used energy is a challenge that recently appeared with the increased use of neural networks, especially in «Deep Learning,» where large models that may contain millions of «neurons» are trained for long periods of time. Training one of these models may require energy that an entire city would consume in a few days[6]. It is one of the shortcomings facing Artificial Intelligence development today. With only 20 volts, the electrical capacity needed by the human brain, a person can learn what one of these models cannot do.

1.6.1 Quantum Computing

In the last ten years, research activity has increased in a new field called «quantum computing,» which is based on «quantum physics», the core of modern physics. High hopes are resting on quantum computing for a quantum leap not only in the field of Artificial Intelligence but in almost every field of science and industry. Quantum computing is distinguished by its ability to process data in parallel so that some of the algorithms used in Artificial Intelligence will become thousands or maybe millions of times faster.

Although several years have passed since the beginning of research on quantum computing, it is so far under development and prototype prototypes. No quantum computers have yet emerged that could be sold commercially. However, upon the

---

6 David Cox at a lecture in MIT 2020.

success of these prototypes, a new era will begin. Therefore, we have devoted some chapters to quantum computing later in this book.

1.7 Artificial Intelligence Domains

If the purpose of Artificial Intelligence research is to create a smart machine that simulates or surpasses humans, fields of Artificial Intelligence cover almost everything that a person can do. There are different foundations to classify Artificial Intelligence topics, including classification on the basis of the approach used to deal with each topic and classification on the basis of the target application of topic. However, all these classifications almost intersect because people themselves use all kinds of intelligence together. In the next paragraphs, we will try to focus on the most important domains or tasks that research and applications focus on, which are the foundations for all other tasks and domains. Under each domain, different topics and classifications of Artificial Intelligence may intersect.

1.7.1 Natural Language Processing (NLP)

NLP is one of the oldest domains of Artificial Intelligence; in fact, even the «Turing Test»[7] is actually a language processing test. Google, a web search engine, is one of the oldest and most important applications of NLP.

---

[7] Alan Turing is a British scientist, a pioneer of computer science, and inventor of the Turing machine, which is one of the first «general purpose» computer models.

The «Turing Test» was named after its founder, English mathematician Alan Turing, who initially intended to find a way to test whether a machine was «smart» or not. In this test, a person interrogates, through a chat program, two other parties, one who is human and the other an Artificial Intelligence program. If that person was not able to identify which of the two parties is the program and which is human, the program would then be considered «smart».

NLP covers several sections, including content-based searches, semantic-based searches (for example, when you search Google for «Artificial Intelligence», it will show results for «Machine Learning» and «neural networks»), language translation, content classification, semantic analysis, summarization, and many other applications.

Likewise, this section includes voice-processing technology, whether «Text to Speech» or «Speech to Text,» which is called «Speech Recognition.» You may well know the applications of this technology, which include «Alexa» from Amazon, «Siri» from Apple, and «Cortana» from Microsoft.

Though it falls under language processing category, speech technology has almost become an independent domain because it is focused on by universities, institutions, and companies, and it has military and security applications which have been in use for decades.

1.7.2 Computer Vision

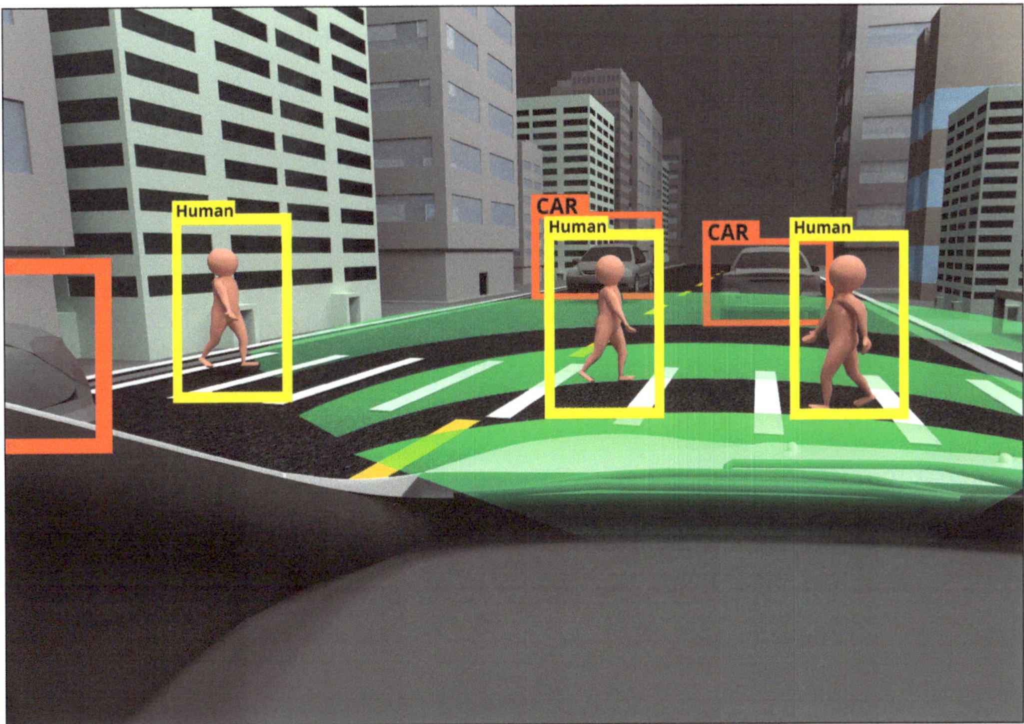

Figure 1.6: Self-driving cars use Computer Vision to identify humans and objects around them.

Computer vision is an attempt by a machine to understand static and successive images (i.e. videos) as understood by humans, whether taken from one camera, multiple cameras, or even from medical imaging devices. This domain is also one of the most researched and applied domains. Applications of this domain include facial recognition and people tracking systems, which have been in use for decades. Recently, these systems have been used during the coronavirus pandemic to identify potentially infected people who were in close contact with a person that tested positive in a public place or to monitor to what extent social distancing rules are applied in crowded places, such as malls, hotels, restaurants, etc.

1.7.3 Robots

Perhaps we have discussed the beginning of this domain in more detail. It is naturally the oldest domain of Artificial Intelligence research and applications. In the modern era, robots have appeared since the 1980s. Almost every large factory has dozens of robotic arms, such as inside car factories. In the last five years, research to mimic human and animal movement has quickly developed. We now have a robot that can run, carry things, and jump a full round back, and another robot that looks like a dog that works in warehouses and construction sites, among other robots.

This progress was driven by the integration of other artificial industry technologies, such as «computer vision,» with motion techniques so that the robot could find its way inside a warehouse or construction site without colliding with a person or an object.

1.7.4 Symbolic Artificial Intelligence

Symbolic Artificial Intelligence is the main domain with which Artificial Intelligence research began in the 1950s. It remained for a long time the main focus of the efforts made by scientists until they culminated in the emergence of what was then called «expert systems» at the end of the 1970s and the beginning of the 1980s.

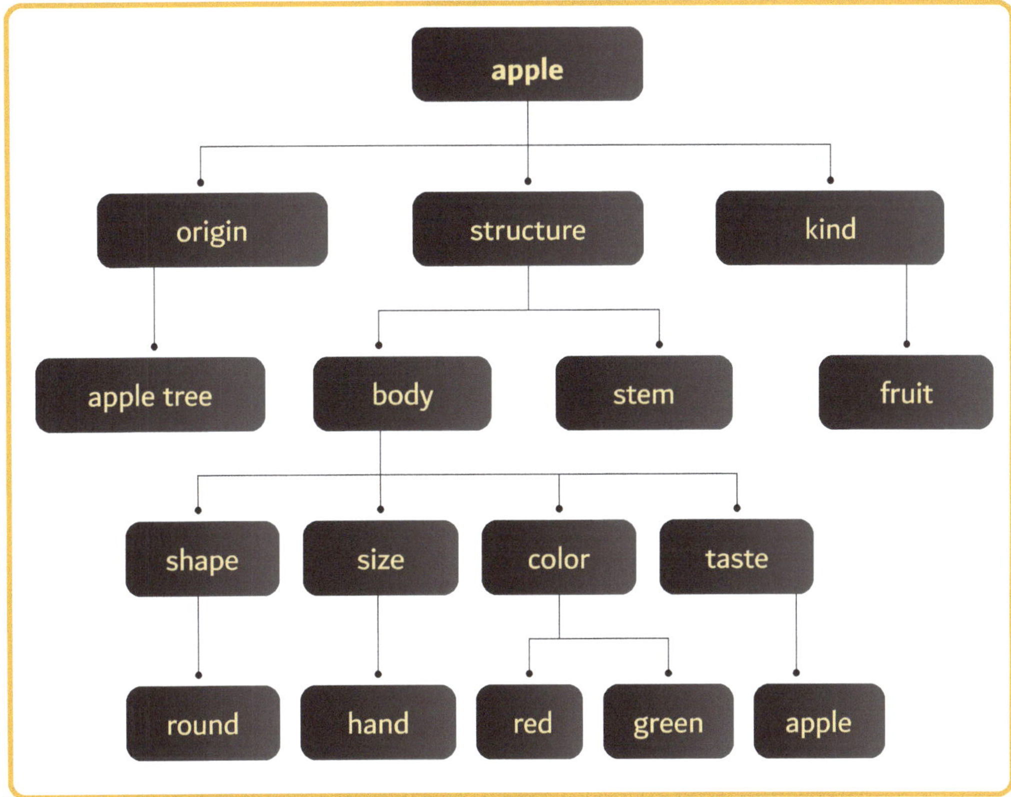

Figure 1.7: An example of how to save an «apple» in a knowledge base

The basic idea of this method is to represent human knowledge in a domain or topic in the form of symbols that people can understand and explain (not digital symbols such as ones used in computer programming, but like those shown above) and then link these symbols in a specific structure to understand the relationships between those symbols.

This structure was used in «expert systems» to represent the rules and facts of a domain and the struvture was called the «knowledge base». It was one of the two parts that formed the expert system, while the other part was the «inference engine» which uses the «knowledge base» to infer new facts.

However, after the spread of these systems and as hopes rose for their development, scientists realized that they can only deal with problems of a limited (knowledge) nature. They fail if the facts and rules to be represented are considerable or difficult to quantify.

1.7.5 Machine Learning

Many non-specialists or even some writers in the field of technology entirely confine Artificial Intelligence to «Machine Learning» which is not correct. In fact, Machine Learning is the subject that finally came to fruition at the beginning of the 21st century with the maturity of «neural networks» that made them practically reliable in various applications. This marked the end of the second «winter» of Artificial Intelligence.

Machine Learning is nearly integrated into every other field of Artificial Intelligence, because it is, in itself, a method or a way, rather than an application. It is included in Natural Language Processing, computer vision, etc. Perhaps the most prominent title under this field is «Deep Learning,» which is the main reason for the great momentum that we see behind the applications of Artificial Intelligence. Therefore, we have devoted an entire chapter to Machine Learning.

CHAPTER 2

DATA

2.1 Oil of the 21st Century

This term probably appeared during the last decade and became very popular and largely accepted. It expressed a general trend in the field of Information Technology to make data the focus of various applications on websites or smartphones. There was also a need to manufacture devices and equipment to store large amounts of data and develop the software necessary to protect that data, most importantly software of data visualization and data analytics.

In fact, data and information were and still are the winning horse, even before the existence of Information Technology. The experienced merchant, who has enough information about the market he trades in, is the one who would win and continue to win even if he started with little capital. An army with the more information is the one that could defeat the other other army, even if the latter was better equipped in terms of soldiers and weapons.

The importance of data is highlighted for several reasons that we are going to look at in the next few paragraphs.

2.2 Big Data

Imagine the information you know about a friend or a relative when you simply browse the general information on their different social networks accounts, then compare that with the information that you could have known about the same person 15 years ago. It was perhaps an achievement then to know the company or organization they worked for. Nowadays, you can know their mood from their status on Facebook.

If you are an employee or a manager at a large company, then you would have definitely heard your fellow technology consultants talking ceaselessly about digital transformation and its importance to the continuity of the company's business and competitive advantage. If, on the other hand, you are working in the public sector, there would be some KPI for the transformation to a digital government or smart government.

Digital transformation actually began with the availability and spread of data storage and management systems, followed by operation management systems within companies and organizations in the mid-1980s. Consequently, reliance on these electronic systems has accelerated, leading now to the concept of paperless transactions and procedures. At the center of all this is the digital integration between and within public and private organizations. Moreover, integrating social platforms into the organizations' systems is one of the important aspects which digital transformation's «enhanced customer experience» strategies focus on. Social platforms are essential interfaces for customers and users to access these organizations' services.

This tremendous development in both directions was accompanied by an ever-increasing growth in the volume of stored data. What made this possible was the development of a server's processing capabilities and the availability of cheap data storage. Every «like» on social networks, every view of a post, and every comment is stored. Every visit by an Amazon customer to a product page is recorded. In addition, images and videos are uploaded every second on these different platforms.

Moreover, with the spread of paperless transactions within organizations, every piece of data is stored in each organization's databases: your contact with customer service, your visit to a branch, services you requested, your financial transactions, complaints you submitted, each product within a warehouse, its exact place, its available quantities, when a product was distributed and to which agency or branch, which sales manager sold what quantity of this product to which customer and what is the category of that customer, and so on.

All this structured data, such as databases, and unstructured data, such as images, videos, tickets, bills and medical reports, are what we call «Big Data».

2.3 Big Data Processing Cycle

Remember the knowledge pyramid? This pyramid is a symbol of human development and transfer of knowledge and wisdom between successive generations. However, in the era of Big Data and supercomputers, the process of building the pyramid must accelerate and change, as if we have gathered multiple (successive) generations of experts and wise persons in one place and with one mind.

2.3 Big Data Processing Cycle

Scientists have developed a cycle with specific steps to process big data. It is a process of data maturation so that the different levels of the knowledge pyramid can be extracted.

The different steps of the «Big Data Cycle» are as follows:

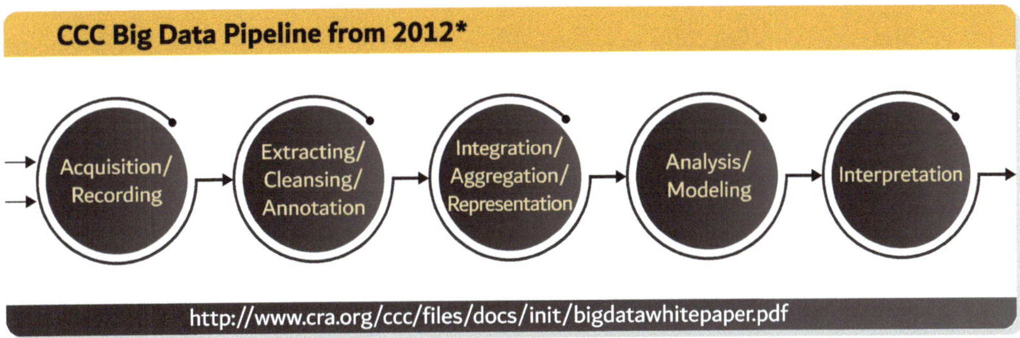

Figure 2.1: Big Data Processing Cycle

1. Data Source Selection and Registration

Data exists in everything surrounding us. Indeed, people's names are a type of data, as well as their height and weight, car's speed, date of product purchases, chest X-rays, etc. What matters in this step is selecting data sources that are related to the context of our work. For example, a customer's eye color, if registered in the database of a shopping website, would not make a difference unless the website sold glasses and contact lenses. Meanwhile, a customer's age is one of the basic determinants that a shopping website needs for advertising and targeting customer segments purposes.

2. Data Extraction and Revision

Data quality varies depending on the efficiency of the systems used. If there are multiple data sources, we may obtain different and conflicting copies of the same data field (for example: the passport number of an airline customer may differ if the customer is issued a new passport or if the data entry clerk commits a mistake). The result of this step is «data» as defined in the knowledge pyramid.

3. Data Integration and Representation

Data of a customer may exist in databases of different systems within the same organization. For example, in an automotive company, the customer data would be found in the Customer Relationship Management (CRM) system, automotive maintenance system, accounting system. etc. In order to have a complete and consistent copy of customer data, various records of the same customer from all those systems must be integrated. We can call that integrated record customer data «information» according to the knowledge pyramid.

4. Data Analysis and Modeling

We use the «integrated revised selected» data to build an analytical knowledge model. After integrating the customers' data, we can build a model that says, for example: **«Clients aged 30-35, who work in administrative positions higher than department manager and live in district X, prefer to buy**

large sedans, whose prices range between $20,000 and $25,000.» This is the knowledge level in our pyramid.

5. Data Interpretation

This can also be called «wisdom extraction» or the decision-making support step. After studying knowledge models that were built in the previous step, the company may make a decision to **«double the production of sports cars in countries where the percentage of young people (15-35 years old) exceeds 65% of the population.»**

2.4 Data Warehouses

If we want to understand the difference between 'databases' and 'data warehouses,' we have to look at big stores like IKEA. Each IKEA branch has a large store, where shelves of that branch are filled directly from that store. Nevertheless, there is one or more large, separate warehouses of the company that supply goods to several branches simultaneously. Goods that each branch needs are transferred from the warehouses to the branch store.

Each store has goods needed by its branch. Goods inside the store are arranged in a way so that they are placed in their display places quickly and with minimal effort (for example: assembling some pieces of furniture such as a desk or table to be ready for display). As for warehouses, they need larger spaces and different organization methods that suit the huge sizes and quantities of goods. Here, there is no need to assemble products or goods, as they could be left packed.

The same applies to data warehouses, as they collect data from various systems databases (similar to the suppliers in the case of warehouses) and reassemble them according to the Big Data Cycle mentioned above to become ready to build analytical models. They are the «single version of the truth» within the organization. As mentioned in a previous example, you will find one revised and integrated copy of the customer data within the data warehouse.

2.5 Data Science

Some people may find that it is difficult to differentiate between «Artificial Intelligence» and «data science». So, let's try together to find that difference.

All concepts that we mentioned in this chapter are closely related to «data science,» in addition to mathematics, statistics, and data visualization. «Data science» is everything that is related to data processing, starting from its extraction from its sources to its presentation and analysis.

The following table[8] (Table 2.1) contains data, specifications, and prices of some houses in a region.

---

8 «AI for Everyone» course, Andrew Ng

If we give this data to data scientists, they will tell us the following:

«Three-room houses are more expensive than two-room ones within the same area. And 'Newly renovated houses' are 15% more expensive than their counterparts.»

House Area (sq ft)	# Rooms	# Bathrooms	Newly Renovated	Price (thousand dollars)
523	1	2	No	115
645	1	3	No	150
708	2	1	No	210
1034	3	3	Yes	280
2290	4	4	No	355
2545	4	5	Yes	440

Table 2.1: Examples of data of some houses

On the other hand, Machine Learning and Artificial Intelligence engineers will convert that data into a predictive model. So, if this model is given this data, it will predict the price of a house. A Machine Learning engineer can also provide you with a model that can deliver the best specifications of a house (as an output) you can buy if you state your budget (as an input.)

2.6 Internet of Things (IoT)

The American researcher, Dr. Neil Gross, Chair of the Department of Sociology at Colby College in the United States, predicted at the end of the 1990s that, «In the next century, planet Earth will don an electronic skin. It will use the Internet as a scaffold to support and transmit its sensations.» This seems to have become a reality today.

You are now in your self-driving car returning home from work. En route, the car calculates the time to reach your home as it uses Google Maps and a traffic congestion estimation feature. Ten minutes before you reach home, the car notifies the «Home Manager» of your arrival. Accordingly, the «Home Manager» turns on the air conditioner and sets the temperature to that which you usually set. It then turns on the TV and sets the appropriate channel according to your favorite program schedule. However, on this day, there is an important match that you want to watch on the sports channel. When you enter your home, you call the «Home Manager» and give an order: «Sports channel». The TV then switches to the «Sports channel» and adjusts the lighting settings in the living room to suit the view. Before the second half begins, the «Home Manager» alerts you that a scheduled call with a customer is approaching, according to the appointment registered on your mobile phone's calendar, and so on and so forth. This is non-fiction. You may have already lived some parts of it or know of it. It is a story of an IoT application, the «Smart Home». The «Home Manager» may be «Google Home», «Amazon Alexa» or other similar devices or applications.

Parts of Smart Home, like all other IoT applications, are still being developed and integrated to create complete systems that many people dream of applying in their homes. Some of these devices and applications are already in use, and others are under development or awaiting technical capabilities such as 5G networks.

2.6.1 What is IoT?

Let's go back to Dr. Gross' speech on the electronic skin of the earth. Just as the human skin is composed of millions of cells that are stitched together, transmit information about the outside world, feel coldness, heat, pain, and pressure, and act as a shield to prevent penetration of the body, electronic skin consists of millions of embedded electronic measuring devices that act as a smart network, collecting and sharing information and data without interruption. Electronic skin performs tasks that have been limited to humans throughout history, such as analyses, forecasting, and decision-making. This network - or the technological concept - is called the Internet of Things (IoT).

The IoT, thus, is everything that is connected to the internet, including humans themselves. Wearing modern watches that measure your vital signs and recognize your geographical location has already made you a part of the IoT network.

Self-driving cars are one of the most important IoT applications. Surveillance cameras, weather sensors in observatories, electronic collars attached to your pet's neck to find its locations, and even parking sensors that inform you of vacancies in parks are part of the IoT network.

Simply put, the Internet of Things is a system of interconnected physical devices that communicate via the Internet. These IoT devices collect, share, generate, and process data in order to improve decision-making and operation automation.

The term «Internet of Things» (IoT) was first coined in 1999 by Kevin Ashton, the British technology pioneer who cofounded the Auto-ID Center at MIT and was a part of the team that helped develop radio-frequency identification (RFID). RFID depends on a device that contains a silicon chip and an antenna so that it can receive and transmit data from «anything», whether a person, an animal, or a machine.

2.6.2 Big Data & 5G Networks

If we want to identify the main factors that have made the «Internet of Things» a reality, we have to consider two factors. The first is related to the development of sensors during the last decade and the reduction of their sizes to a degree that enables them to be placed inside watches, clothes, and other small or large devices. The second is the development of wireless communication so that these sensors and devices can send data they have collected to specialized processing programs for analysis before sending the result instantaneously to the concerned parties, whether human beings or other devices.

When we spoke about big data, most of our writing was about data sources related to the direct activities of human beings, such as social networking sites, interactive platforms, and government and corporate systems. However, in light of the Internet of Things revolution and estimates by experts that the number of devices connected to virtual IoT networks exceeds 20 billion devices [9] in 2020, the largest part of big data will be from what is collected from those devices and sensors. The size of the data that may be collected from the activities of a given person on a day, such as card payments for purchases, and data that a person enters into company

[9] MIT Technology Review

systems, emails, and posts shared on Facebook may not exceed the size of a video that the camera, placed by the same person on the door of his «Smart Home,» would record in an hour. It may also not exceed the size of data that his smart watch will collect on his vital signs during the same day.

Hence, it is important to have highly efficient wireless networks that can transmit this huge data and also ensure that this data instantaneously reaches its destination with high accuracy without errors. Surgeons in Japan performing a precise procedure using a surgical robot located in the United States can perform this procedure only through a high speed data transfer network that ensures the patient's image instantaneously reaches Japan from the United States. It must also transmit control signals of the surgical robot back-forward and at the same speed without errors. Without this high speed network, the robot and the IoT network that links the robot to the surgeon can't be linked together.

There are multiple examples of similar applications that require the same capabilities. Accordingly, the competition between countries to create and control 5G networks is at its most intense because this would mean controlling the future and ensuring strategic, economic, and social superiority.

2.6.3 Smart Cities

«Smart Home» is an important IoT application; «Smart City» is more important.

Smart cities are one of the most important pillars of sustainable development plans. They - like smart homes - are based on connecting and integrating all facilities of these cities and data flow from all sectors and facilities of the city to data processing clouds and Artificial Intelligence tools.

In the transportation sector, self-driving cars will become - perhaps - the only cars. Cars that exchange data among each other, perhaps eliminating the need for traffic lights, or they will exchange data with the city's infrastructure to know the best routes to their destination. This would not be just to avoid traffic congestion, but perhaps to reduce visual and audio pollution in some areas, avoid school areas when students leave school, or because the car needs to be recharged before it reaches its destination, among other possibilities.

In the energy sector, one of the goals of smart cities is to utilize solar energy through relatively small panels that are installed in public places, on roofs, and even above seats in parks. The rationalization of energy consumption by installing light and movement sensors around the city and inside homes and organizations, as well as processing data collected by these sensors, will contribute to the rationalization of energy use. It may even contribute to future planning for each city's energy needs, perhaps day by day.

You may have heard or read about studies on the spread of COVID-19. Data included in these studies were collected from samples taken from the sewage in some neighborhoods and cities. This method of using sewage water and other forms of infrastructure is at the core of Smart City technologies. Sensors that continuously collect data from a sewage and then process that data using Artificial Intelligence techniques may be one of the most important factors in preventing the spread of epidemics in the future, either by anticipating their spread or controlling the areas of their outbreak. The matter may go beyond that to the ability to study the prevailing lifestyles in every neighborhood and city. This will lead to decisions that improve lifestyles for residents of those cities.

As we indicated at the beginning, data is the real wealth and main source for building a civilization at the present time. Data outweighs the importance of oil for the Industrial Revolution at its beginning.

CHAPTER 3

MACHINE LEARNING

3.1 Can a Machine Learn?

«Let's start by telling the truth: machines don't learn. What a typical 'learning machine' does, is finding a mathematical formula, which, when applied to a collection of inputs (called 'training data'), produces the desired outputs.»[10]

Yes, machines or computers do not learn, but by using different **algorithms**, we can try to create a «mathematical equation,» or a **model** whose variables are estimated from the available data on which the machine is **trained**. Then, we use this mathematical equation with the new data to produce an output that represents the predicted or inferred value.

Do you remember the example of the houses in the previous chapter when we used the houses' data? This data represents here the training data. We try to find a mathematical equation whose inputs are: house area, number of rooms, number of bathrooms, and whether the house was recently renovated. The output of the equation would be the price of the house.

This is the simplest possible way to describe Machine Learning. We can also define it, in light of the knowledge pyramid, as the process of encapsulating wisdom in a

---

10 Andrei Burkov- «The Hundred-Page Machine Learning Book»

mathematical model. The «learning machine» is almost mimicking an expert in one field, e.g. real estate, who has years of experience that provides him access to thousands of housing data points. This enables him to estimate the price of any house based on its data.

Accordingly, Machine Learning goes through two stages. The first is the **model building stage** by learning from data, i.e. finding the mathematical formula that is compatible with data. The second is the **model use stage**, or, in other words, the stage of deploying the model to a real environment as a product that can be used.

In the first stage, we use algorithms to build a model. These algorithms are numerous and diverse and often rely on statistical and mathematical foundations, the most famous of which is «neural networks.» This phrase has become synonymous with the term «Machine Learning.»

3.2 Neural Networks and Deep Learning

Neural networks are an attempt by scientists to simulate a network of neurons that make up the human brain. They consist of neurons or «nerve nodes,» where each neuron is linked to other neurons through neurotransmitters or «axons» that transmit electrical signals between these neurons. Mathematical simulations of these networks produce a very complex mathematical model, making it capable of dealing with complex problems in Artificial Intelligence.

An artificial neural network is an interconnected group of nodes - or points - that are stacked in layers behind each other, as indicated in Figure 3.1b. Apart from the mathematical foundations, the so-called **«Deep Learning»** is to have a neural network with more layers rather than a single layer such as the one indicated in Figure 3.1b.

Biological Neuron versus Artificial Neural Network

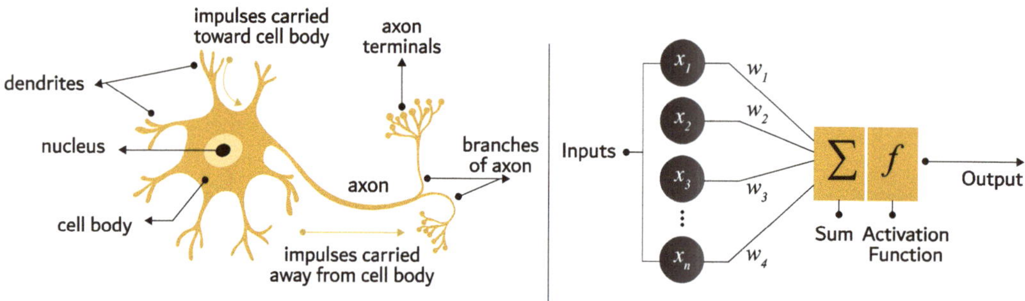

Figure 3.1: A- Human neural network B- Artificial neural network

You most likely have used a facial recognition program, whether to unlock your smartphone or to post your photo with your friends tagged on Facebook. If such a program works with a **Deep Learning** model, this model would be composed of several layers, the first layer recognizing shapes such as lines and circles, while the second identifies structures from outputs of the first layer (for example, the eye consists of a line that represents eyebrows, the oval shape represents the pupils, and the circle represents the iris). Finally, the third layer can recognize the combination of outputs of the second layer, which is the face. Accordingly, the identity of a person who has that face can then be matched.

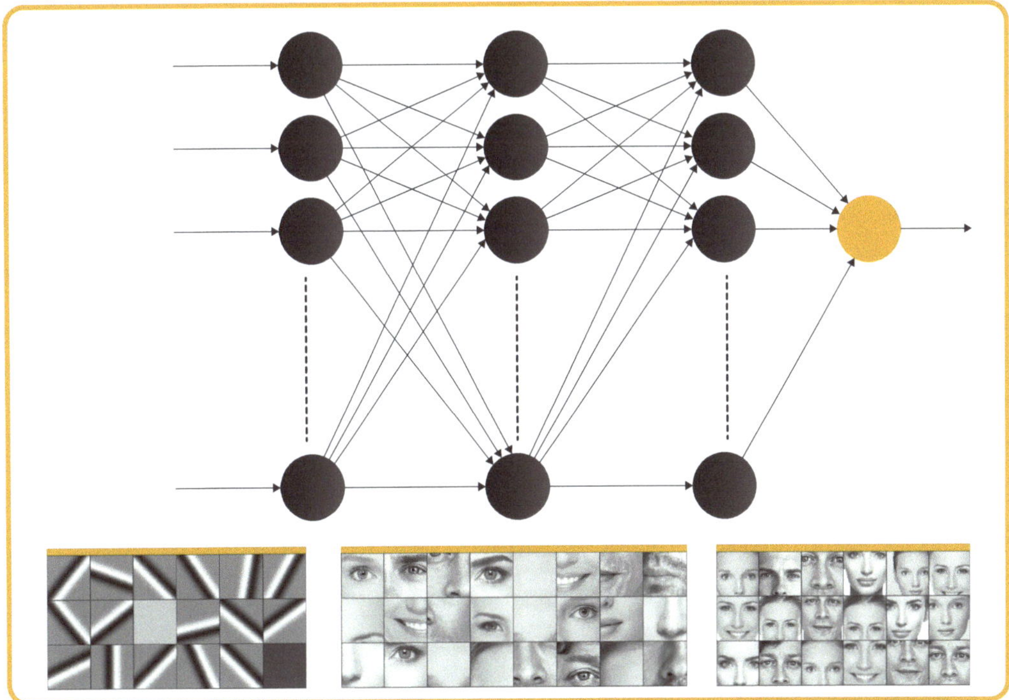

Figure 3.2: Neural networks and an example of how they can be used in face recognition.

3.3 Types of Machine Learning

There are basic types of learning under the heading «Machine Learning,» which are the building blocks with which an integrated system that works with Artificial Intelligence can be built. Each type can be built by different algorithms. «Neural network» is the most commonly used one.

3.3.1 Supervised Learning

«Supervised learning» produces models that are trained on what is called "labeled data." This means that we obtain data that contains inputs and outputs (labels), such as the data of houses. This data contains specifications of houses as inputs and prices of houses as outputs (or labels). Through those outputs (or labels), we «supervise» the machine on how to learn from the input data. Supervised learning is divided into two types or intended to perform two tasks:

1. **Classification**

If you were given a set of car images, you can classify them, for example, into two classes: 1- passenger cars and 2- trucks. However, we need to teach the «machine» how to identify both classes. We need to enter images of cars labeled with passenger cars and trucks to teach it how to differentiate between the two classes.

This also applies to educating the machine how to discover bone fractures from the patients' X-rays. In this case, there are two classes: fracture or no fracture. Machines can also learn multi-classes classification tasks such as identifying a group of animal species from their images.

2. **Regression**

Instead of predicting a type, a machine predicts a number that fits the input data, as is the case in the example of the houses where the machine predicts the price of the house from its specifications, estimates the age of people from photos of their faces, or forecasts the temperature based on weather data and more.

3.3.2 Unsupervised Learning

When a machine learns from «unlabeled» training data to perform specific tasks, «unsupervised learning» takes place, the most important of which are presented[11] below:

1. Clustering

If we gave a machine a set of students' data and asked the machine to distribute them in a specified number of clusters, and the entered data were as follows:

- Age
- Classroom
- Favorite subject
- Average score of the last 3 years
- Height
- Weight
- Home address

---

11 We did not mention other important types such as «density estimation» and «dimensionality reduction» because they require technical explanations that go beyond the scope of this book. You can refer to other resources such as Andriy Burkov's «The Hundred-Page Machine Learning Book».

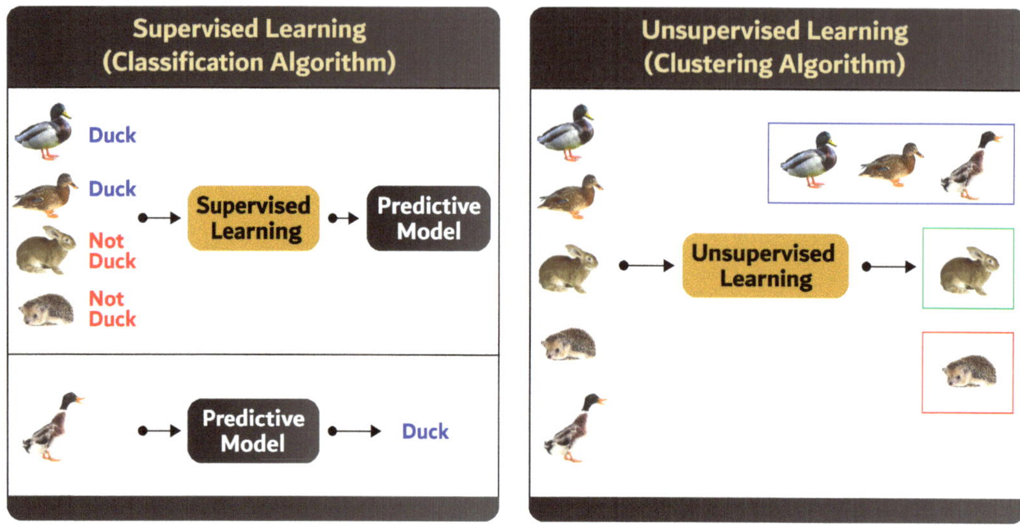

Figure 3.3: Comparison between Supervised Learning (Classification) and Unsupervised Learning (Clustering)

The machine would try to find a scale upon which it could put similar students into the same cluster. It would perhaps use a composite scale of height, weight, and age, or a scale consisting of the home address and age, etc.

2. Anomaly Detection (Outlier Detection)

Thousands or perhaps millions of financial transactions take place every day within a bank (card payments, transfers between accounts, etc.), but some of these transactions may be «fraudulent.» Therefore, relying on a principle of «classification» to detect these transactions may not be accurate or effective due to the lack of available data about fraudulent transactions compared to the trusty and normal transactions. What is the solution?

Here comes the technique of «outlier detection,» which tries to find the operations which do not resemble most of the normal operations that occur every day in the bank. The same technique is applied to discovering computer network intruders. By parsing through the millions of data transfer operations that take place within a network, the suspected ones are discovered, and the network administrators are alerted to take action.

3.4 Reinforcement Learning

Do you remember how you learned chess? You may have started learning the basic rules, but then, while you were playing with a friend, you learned some «tricks,» and these tricks meant you took some steps that might seem useless until checkmating your opponent. Over time, your sophistication, mastery of trickery, and ability to improvise increased with each new «situation» or «state» your opponent had put you in.

In «reinforcement learning,» we try to push the machine to learn to perform some tasks in the same way we did when learning chess. Indeed, we learn tricks if they succeed, and leave and forget tricks if they fail. We learn that the current step, even if it appears to be a failure, will lead to the ultimate goal. At the end, for example, you may sacrifice a pawn to attack the queen.

In «reinforcement learning» we put machines in the learning environment, which is the chess game, and then we use the carrot and stick method.

If the step taken by the machine leads to a loss, we give it a negative score. However, if it leads to a success, we give it a positive score. The stronger the step is, whether negative or positive, the greater the size of the penalty or reward respectively. And the goal of the machine during the learning process is to collect the highest positive amount of rewards.

Applications of «reinforcement learning» include, of course, many areas other than games. They may be involved in operating self-driving vehicles or controlling traffic. They are an essential component of robot «brains» in general.

Many experts predict that «reinforcement learning» will become the strongest and most widely used type of Machine Learning in the near future.

CHAPTER 4

DIGITAL TRANSFORMATION

4.1 Digital Transformation

This is among the most famous topics in the last five years. The COVID-19 pandemic made it even more prominent, but before that, different factors led to the acceleration of digital transformation within organizations during the last decade.

In fact, digital transformations started from the 1980s with the spread of computers, especially personal computers, when their purchase was no longer limited to rich governments or large companies anymore. Then there are software companies who spread and develop systems to help companies organize their databases and gradually. the scope of these systems eventually expanded to cover almost every detail in the business of any organization or company today.

During the last decade, 3G, 4G, and 5G communication networks appeared, which eased and accelerated data exchange. In addition, those networks have become stronger, more stable, and more reliable in providing access to websites and electronic platform services without interruption. At the same time, smartphones have become ubiquitous among adults all day and in every place. Millions of applications have spread to meet all the needs of different people. We should not forget details mentioned in Chapter 2 about the availability of data and big data. Most importantly, many types of technology such as «Internet of things,» «Artificial Intelligence,» and «blockchain» have emerged and provided opportunities for various organizations and companies to develop their businesses in a way that was impossible before. And so accordingly, these organizations and companies have placed technology and electronic systems at the heart of their business.

What Is Digital Transformation?

Digital transformation simply occurs when «technology leads the organization business tendencies!» Yes, it is that simple a term. Until recently, IT departments were placed within the organization hierarchy under the «Shared Services» group, which meant they were placed along with administrative and maintenance departments which are not part of the organizations' core business. And at times, an external company might have been contracted to carry out the Information Technology work within the organization.

Now, positions such as «Chief Information Officer» (CIO) are considered key positions within the organization. These positions were even subdivided into other positions such as «Chief Technology Officer» (CTO) and «Chief Data Officer» (CDO), to reflect the extent of an organization's reliability on Information Technology.

Before we reached this level of digital transformation, communication of any organization with its customers was through employees who were working in real, physical customer service outlets and dealt with the organization's systems to fulfil customer's requests. A customer's opportunity to use the organization's systems or services electronically was almost absent. However, with the emergence of online shopping (eCommerce) websites, a new concept, so-called «self-service,» has emerged.

In any eCommerce website, a customer reviews products, adds them to the basket, selects method of shipping, and pays for those products without interference of any employee of the operator company. These tasks provided by «self-service» originally required several employees working on several systems in a physical outlet until completion of the purchase process.

Do you remember when you needed an account statement for the last six months from your bank? Before, you had to visit one of the bank's physical branch and fill out an application form, then a customer service agent would send it to the Information Technology department to print and send it back to the branch where you could collect it. Today, you can download the statement in just few seconds from the bank's mobile application. Moreover, you can open a new account without visiting the bank for several times like you used to!

Based on the above, we can summarize the most important areas of «digital transformation» as follows:

- **Enhancing Customer Experience:** You can now order a pizza from Domino's Pizza through ten different channels, including WhatsApp and Facebook. You can also design your wardrobe and pay for it on IKEA's website.
- **Omni-Channel (Standardization and Integration of Organization's Channels):** Whether it is a profitable organization like companies or a service organization like government agencies, all customer service channels must be integrated. Maintenance requests that arrive through customer service call centers must appear on the customer's account on the company

website or the smartphone application. In addition, you can follow up with the maintenance engineer's arrival through said application by connecting the engineer's phone number to the operations center of that company.

- **Data Flow and Analysis Services:** As we mentioned in the chapter on data, data collection from its various sources within the organization has become a fundamental pillar of an organization's business. Implementation of the «Big Data Cycle» will improve the «customer experience» and ensure data flow between the different «channels» in the organization.

- **New Technology Tracking and Rationalization:** Almost every month, a new technology appears. It probably becomes a «trend» that everyone is talking about and trying to integrate into their organization. However, in any organization, there must be an entity that defines its digital transformation strategy and indicates how to utilize any new technology without wasting the organization resources.

Let's conclude here with an imaginary example. A customer of a pizza company expressed their dissatisfaction with the delivery service through a post on their Facebook page. The company's sentimental analysis system, which incorporates an Artificial Intelligence system, alerted the employee in charge that there is a problem with a customer. The employee responded to the customer to inquire about the reason of the problem. Meanwhile, the employee entered the Customer Relationship Management system, used data analysis tools, and found that the customer used to request «X» pizza the most times, so the employee created a discount coupon for this type of pizza and put it in his response to the comment on the Facebook post as a compensation from the company to maintain its reputation in front of other customers.

4.2 Enterprise Architecture and Transformation Management

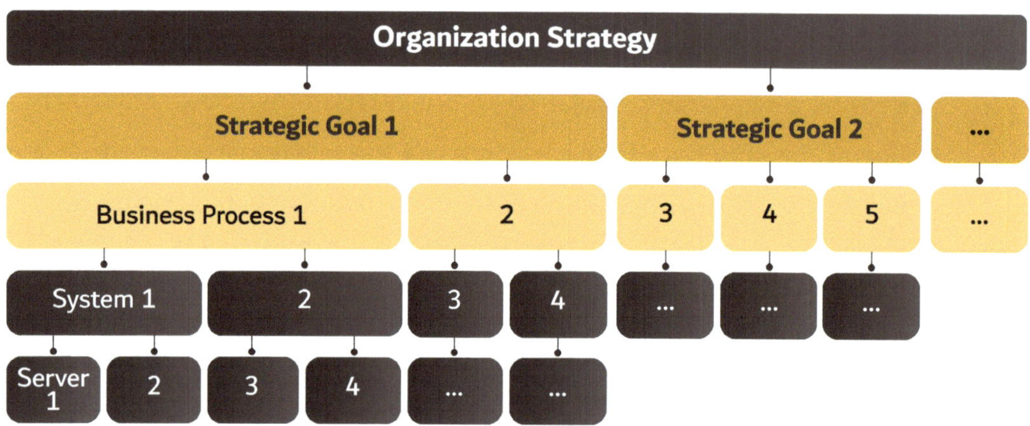

Figure 4.1: Holistic View of an Organization through Concepts of Enterprise Architecture

As mentioned in the previous section of this chapter, the roles of Chief Information/ Technology Officers have been upgraded during the last decade to become central roles within any organization and have acquired an important representation within the organization strategy office by EA architects.

Enterprise Architecture (EA) is a framework and procedural process that looks at the organization in a holistic manner. It enables the organization to create its current blueprint and develop and design future ones as well. It aims to achieve the strategic goals of the organization by aligning the organization's business with its Information Technology.

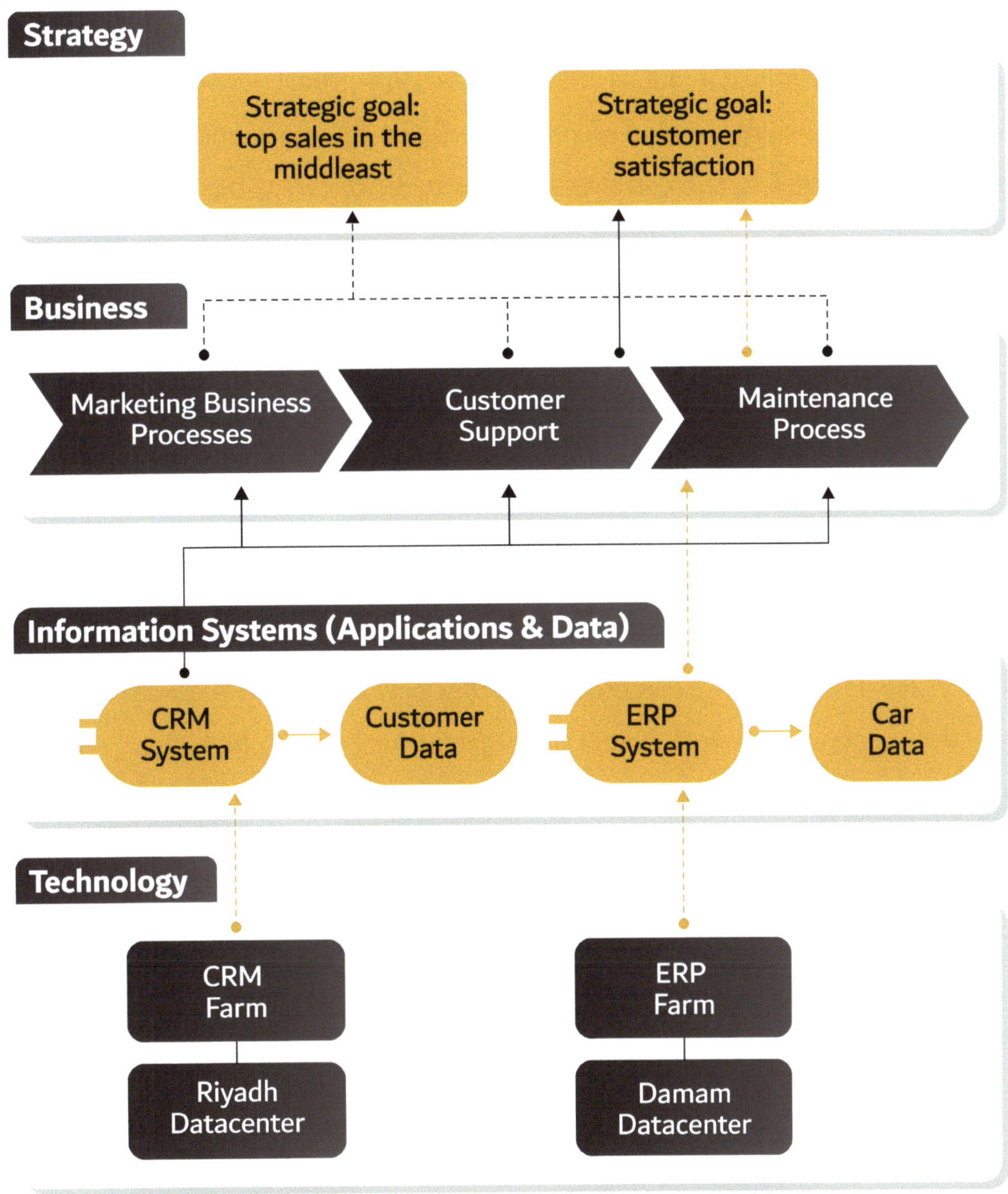

Figure 4.2: (Imaginary) Enterprise Architecture Blueprint of a Company Selling and Maintaining Cars

EA activities span the area between strategy and operations. They consider an organization's strategic goals as the organization's primary inputs. From these goals, initiatives emerge, on top of which are digital transformation initiatives. As indicated in Figure 4.1, each strategic goal requires different business processes to be achieved, and a strategic goal may share one or more common processes with another goal. In turn, the different processes may share one or more electronic systems to automate those processes. Each system needs servers, networks and other appliances to operate.

4.2.1 How does Enterprise Architecture Manage Transformation?

We will use here an example in order to realize how Enterprise Architecture is an effective tool to drive change within the organization by using its holistic view and layered perception of the organization.

A company found that in order to reach the size of its strategically targeted customer base, it had to build branches in all geographical areas where it operated instead of relying solely on external distributors. Therefore, EA architects analyzed the following:

1. Business Processes: There are no specific processes or mechanisms to communicate with retailers, and the introduction of these mechanisms requires the creation of new jobs and modifications to the company structure.

2. Operations: There is no call center or hotline through which customers can communicate with the company.

3. Operations: The current software and databases do not fit the new operational requirements resulting from the establishment of many branches and the change of customer type from only distributors to both distributors and retailers. Thus, there is a steady increase in the number of daily operations on the databases.

4. Operations: The company is relying on a limited infrastructure that serves the main office only. To serve new branches, a data center should be established and means of communication should be extended between the data center and branches.

Hence, this change initiative in company business will turn into a group of projects in multiple fields, such as:

- Administrative project to introduce procedures and mechanisms required for branches to operate
- Human resources project to recruit and hire qualified personnel for new processes and procedures
- Infrastructure and communication project
- Project to modify, build, and purchase necessary software for branches and call center to operate

- Finance project to introduce financial operations that cover new and different operations and clients

Then, EA architects organize these projects in a series of successive initiatives (transition architectures) to reach the final objectives. This sequence ensures that the company business is not negatively affected by the transformation.

4.3 Transformation Streams

The spread and reliance on technology has led to an increase in investments in technology. As a result, tech giants have become the top valued companies with the largest market value across the world. The capital of some giants has exceeded one trillion dollars.

But the dominance of technology also has disadvantages. Wherever the money is concentrated, the press, media, and marketing companies surround it. Technology press is now strongly present in all media channels. News and rumors about technology companies are the main engine of financial markets and attract audience and readers, even those who are not technology specialists. Therefore, one disadvantage is that the decision makers in large organizations and companies are exposed to the news that unreasonably promotes some technology before it reaches a safe level of maturity. This has often resulted in organizations wasting their initiatives and budget on new technologies that are doomed to failure in the end, or even spending money on non-applicable technology instead of waiting until the technology matures and costs are reduced.

So, what are the main streams of transformation within the organization?

Human Resources, Business Processes, and Tools and Systems.

In order for any change or transformation attempt to succeed within the organization, those in charge of change must work on the three streams of human resources, business processes, and tools and systems together. Otherwise, the attempt would most likely fail.

Through my experience, the most important cause of failure of transformation initiatives in organizations is the negligence of human resources and the focus on tools and systems. In fact, some organizations hurry to spend huge sums on purchasing softwares, systems, and tools, as the decision makers assume that these advanced technological systems are the magical solution to any problem they may face. This is usually the result of the continuous momentum of the media or suppliers who are trying to make profits by any means necessary.

Artificial Intelligence should not be a goal in itself for any organization. Directions of the top management cannot be that Artificial Intelligence should be used in our work in any way in order to keep pace with universal evolution and compete with other companies and organizations. Artificial Intelligence must be used in the context of the organization'd transformation initiatives and to achieve its strategic goals in the manner set forth earlier in this chapter.

In the next chapter, we will explore together the transformation roadmap.

CHAPTER 5

ROADMAP

In this chapter, we will establish steps of transformation to Artificial Intelligence and other advanced technologies in any organization. We will not target companies or organizations that are specialized in Artificial Intelligence or any specific technology. Rather, we will target companies and organizations that want to use advanced technologies as a tool to help them achieve their for-profit and non-profit goals.

5.1 Route Reconnaissance

As indicated earlier, the rate of technology development and emergence of new technologies is almost unmatched in any other field of science. Therefore, any organization has to dedicate a position in its strategy or planning departments to be responsible for reconnoitering new technology developments and submit a quarterly report to the head of technology (or even to the board themselves), which addresses the following key elements:

- The new technologies that appeared recently, with a simplified explanation of each technology.
- Status of technologies currently used within the organization, its future, and either its investment feasibility by purchasing new systems or replacing them in case there are indications that they will leave the market.

- Selection of some new technologies to conduct research on them being adopted into the organization.
- Report on competing organizations (or similar organizations in the case of government organizations) in terms of their use of technology and its impact on the organization's competitiveness.

This role is usually performed by Enterprise Architecture specialists with this approach used with some customization in the case of Artificial Intelligence. Keeping track of the various Artificial Intelligence applications has now become an inevitable task and capturing the most suitable one for the organization is no longer a luxury.

5.2 Artificial Intelligence Team

There are always two approaches for any organization to take to build the new capabilities it needs. The first is that the organization should use vendors to meet its requirements for these new capabilities. The second is that the organization should build a reliable internal team to completely perform the required tasks.

In fact, the organization must employ a team, especially with regard to Artificial Intelligence capabilities, which represents the minimum capability to implement Artificial Intelligence projects, given that Artificial Intelligence is still a new field and the market is full of those who claim to have these capabilities. In addition, data privacy requirements of the organization cannot be met without a representative who is responsible for protecting that data on behalf of the organization. Therefore, we recommend forming a specialized team with a minimum number of employees rather than relying on a project manager to manage the project and outsourcing, as is the case in most external projects.

5.2.1 Data Scientist

A data scientist is someone specialized in data and statistics who has the knowledge to implement the «Big Data Cycle» steps indicated in Chapter 2. They can perform data analysis and develop hypotheses to understand insights from data.

5.2.2 Artificial Intelligence Engineer

AI engineer is an expert in building Artificial Intelligence software, especially improving efficiency and accuracy, and rationalizing various models. They are usually a specialist in Machine Learning and Deep Learning and works alongside the data scientist.

5.2.3 Field Expert

Every company or organization has a business scope, e.g. banking, medicine, agriculture, etc. Each field requires an expert who can understand problems and challenges that the organization faces. They must be able to suggest some solutions to improve or reduce risks. This expert is a focal point between the business and Artificial Intelligence team. They act as a translator of, among other things, domain-specific language, data, and Artificial Intelligence language. Therefore, an expert must have sufficient understanding of technology and know how to deal with AI engineers.

5.3 Data Infrastructure

Do you have a mature data infrastructure? Have you applied what we explained in Chapter 2? Do you have one or more data warehouses in your organization? Have you defined a clear policy for data management in the organization? Have you created standards to measure data quality of the databases of different systems?

If your organization has not reached a sufficient degree of maturity in terms of its data management, it may be time to launch an initiative to organize data throughout the organization in line with the «Big Data Cycle.» This cannot be achieved without progress in one of the most important streams of «digital transformation» that have been already indicated in the previous chapter, «Standardization and Integration of Organization's Channels» or «Omni-Channel.»

Artificial Intelligence and Machine Learning almost entirely depend on data, its availability, and its quality. Therefore, Artificial Intelligence should be looked at as an advanced stage of technological maturity of the organization.

5.3.1 Data Architecture Maturity

We can measure the maturity of the organization in terms of data through two main indicators. The first measures the organization's ability to rely on the data in the decision-making processes. This is measured by the accuracy and consistency of this data. The second indicator measures the ability to benefit from that data in terms of the availability of data analysis tools, on top of which are intelligence models.

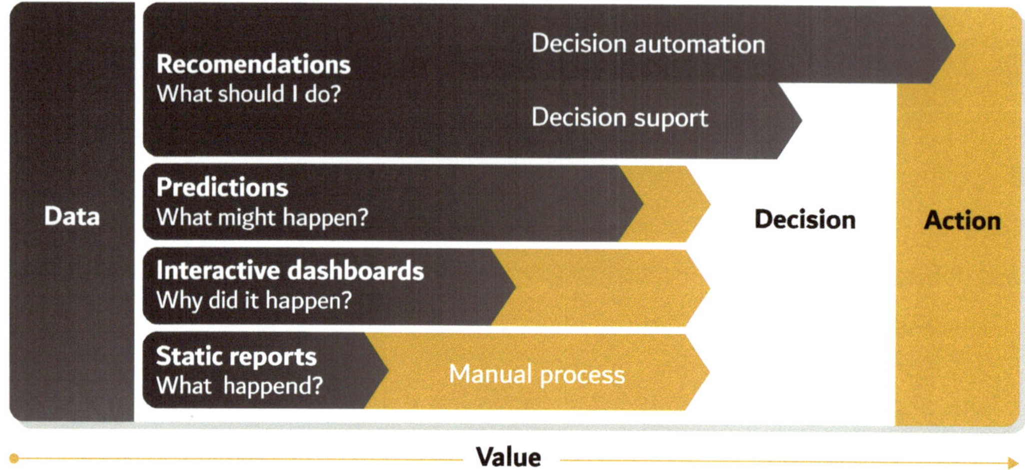

Figure 5.1: The more the organization matures in terms of data, the less it relies on manual work, instead entrusting the work to its systems.

The following five stages represent the levels of maturity of the enterprise data:

1. Static Reports

They are usually reports that are often designed to be printed or attached to some email as a type of periodic reports. They contain lists of records to be reported and some direct statistics. Example: a list of records of houses sold in the first quarter of the current year by the branch located in the city center. This type of report often depends on the database of one system (in the previous example: Sales Management System)

2. Interactive Dashboards

They are interactive dashboards based on aggregated statistics. The user can modify various filters in the dashboard itself to determine factors affecting the targeted statistics. Example: a dashboard that includes the number of houses sold in different years and the prices of those houses, and has the ability to filter these statistics by number of rooms, area of houses, salesmen, age group of the salesman, name of salesman's manager, and names of the branches which completed the sales, with different types of graphs to illustrate these statistics. This level requires the integration of different systems' data (in this example, integration of the sales system, financial system, and human resource system).

3. Predictability

Predictability is, for example, using Artificial Intelligence to predict prices of houses or sales of a salesman during the next year.

4. Decision Support

Decision Support means that the organization's Artificial Intelligence software can provide recommendations to support decision makers within the organization. For example, it can recommend purchasing a number of houses due to their cheaper prices with an opportunity to sell those houses at higher prices in the next year.

5. Decision Automation

Decision making means that the organization's confidence in Artificial Intelligence systems has reached a level that allows these systems to make decisions on its behalf. For example, an Artificial Intelligence software which can update the prices of the houses that are intended to be sold.

5.4 Technology Infrastructure

5.4.1 Computational Power

Training models using complex algorithms such as neural networks and Deep Learning requires powerful computers that may have different specifications than traditional computers.

Traditional computers often rely on classic Central Processing Units (CPUs) that are available in all types of computers, including servers. However, the high computing performance necessary for running these algorithms needs other types of units called «Graphics Processing Units» (GPUs).

GPUs exist in «display cards» and are mainly concerned with exporting graphics to display devices such as monitors. They speed up graphic processing of all kinds, including 3D graphics. GPUs have special capabilities distinguishing them from CPUs in terms of their ability to process large amounts of data in parallel, using advanced and complex built-in electronic circuits not available in CPUs.

Another type of processors, Field Programmable Gate Array (FPGA), appeared later. These processors are unique as they can be programmed according to the task they are intended to perform. Thus, they give flexibility in terms of the nature of tasks they can perform. In addition, they have other capabilities which are similar to GPUs.

Current hopes rest on, as we indicated earlier, the quantum computer. Due to its importance, we have devoted a couple of chapters to it, as decision makers need to know the potential opportunities as well as the challenges that accompany these future computers before making the decision to invest in them.

But apart from the quantum computer, we should also ask: does an organization need to buy devices that have such advanced processors like GPUs and FPGAa?

Both types still have high prices compared to CPUs. Investing in these two types requires a rational plan to avoid wasting organizational resources. It is better for the work team to start relying on cloud services until the increased use of these cloud services is more expenisve to maintain than buying and hosting the advanced processor devoces within the organization data center.

5.4.2 Internet of Things (IoT)

Collecting data from «things» connected to the IoT network is not the main goal of the network rather, as we indicated earlier, analyzing that data and using the results to support and automate decision-making is the ultimate goal of data collection. As explained earlier, the use of Artificial Intelligence techniques in this work represents the highest maturity degree of data analysis systems.

In any organization, a strategy on how to benefit from the concept and technology of «Internet of Things» should be developed. The outcome of this strategy is a technical structure map that shows the devices and sensors that serve objectives and activities of the organization in each section and even their geographical distribution. This structure shows the paths of data flow from those devices and sensors into the organization's data warehouse. Subsequently; data analysis, Artificial Intelligence, and Machine Learning models which can take advantage of these vast amounts of data should be built.

There are types of structures through which «Internet of Things» is integrated with work systems in the organization. Selection of structure depends on the size and types of devices and sensors which the organization possesses. We can summarize the common types of this structure as follows:

- Data may flow directly to data warehouses without processing and will be processed later;

- Data may be processed directly inside advanced devices and sensors which contain microprocessors. Then, results of analysis are transferred to the organization's data warehouse. Recently, researchers at MIT University built an integrated Artificial Intelligence system that can work inside these microprocessors.

- The latest type to start spreading, the Edge Cloud, is an intermediate area in which data is stored and processed after it is collected from sensors and devices. Then, the results of the processing and analysis are submitted to the organization's data warehouses.

The last two types are suitable for the requirements of systems that operate in real time, such as road monitoring systems or patient monitoring systems, which need to process data and make decisions in real time.

5.4.3 Cloud Services

Artificial Intelligence services have become a major component of services provided by cloud service giants, led by Google, Amazon, and Microsoft. In addition, these companies have built open-source software libraries to develop various Artificial Intelligence algorithms, which have greatly contributed to the progress and maturity of the Artificial Intelligence industry as a whole. In the following paragraphs, we will review the most important types of cloud services of Artificial Intelligence:

- **Computational Power**

  As indicated earlier, it is the availability of affordable processors depending on their use.

- **AI-Powered Design Tools**

  They range from coding platforms to easy-to-use graphical user interface tools that beginners or non-professionals can use to develop their Artificial Intelligence capabilities.

- **Artificial Intelligence Competition Platforms**

The most famous of one is «Kaggle,» on which some companies and organizations host competitions where Artificial Intelligence software developers compete to develop high-precision and efficient algorithms. All these services have greatly helped enrich the community of Artificial Intelligence developers.

- **Pre-trained Models and Ready-made AI Software**

These include computer vision softwares where you can, for example, use a few photos of you and your colleagues to have a program recognize your faces in a few minutes, or a Natural Language Processing software where you can use the speech recognition service to transform a conference you are hosting into a live broadcast with subtitles under the speaker's video. These may be even translated instantly into a number of languages.

- **IoT Edge Cloud**

As indicated above, IoT Edge Cloud is an intermediate area for collecting and processing data from sensors and devices. However, it also provides other services that help organizations focus on their business, including data security services, software operating devices and sensors, and Artificial Intelligence services that work directly on data received from devices (such as computer vision models that work directly on images received from the production line surveillance cameras in a factory) and more. These can come from cloud service companies or from other suppliers, including manufacturers of these sensors and devices.

CHAPTER 6

APPLICATIONS OF ARTIFICIAL INTELLIGENCE

We tackled some areas of Artificial Intelligence in chapter 1, such as computer vision and Natural Language Processing. These areas are the basic building blocks that developers and creators of Artificial Intelligence applications use to build their applications by placing them in structures that suit the requirements of each application. Since Artificial Intelligence applications have become so numerous and varied, we will only focus on some of these applications to clarify the Artificial Intelligence systems that achieves the desired goal.

6.1 Recognizing COVID-19 in the Sound of a Cough

At Massachusetts Institute of Technology (MIT), a team of researchers were working on finding a way to diagnose some diseases using a cell phone recording of a patient's cough. Their research included pneumonia as well as Alzheimer, as they weaken the vocal cords due to degradation of the nerves that control them.

With the onset of the COVID-19 pandemic and its associated effects that no person or entity on the earth was spared from, the MIT team decided to assist in the efforts aiming to fight the virus. They have already succeeded in building an Artificial Intelligence model that can identify individuals infected with COVID-19 even if the patients do not have any symptoms, which was one of their most important goals. It is known that those infected individuals who do not show symptoms of infection with COVID-19 are the group that most spreads the virus among others, so their impact and harm may be greater than other groups, since whoever shows symptoms of infection is subject to isolation and thus cannot transmit the disease to others.

How was this model built and how will the application reach people? The model is a Natural Language Processing model that we talked about previously. It specifically belongs to the speech processing and recognition category, such as Apple's «Siri» or Amazon's «Alexa.» However, it of course differs in terms of the goal. It classifies the sound of the user's cough into «infected» or «not infected» instead of converting the user's voice into commands that the app can executes.

The researchers trained the model on cough sounds of volunteers who recorded their sounds through a dedicated page, which a user can access from any device connected to the web. The collected sample sounds contained sounds of COVID-19 patients and healthy people, people who had symptoms, and others who did not have symptoms. Of course, the team was keen on diversifying people in terms of gender, race, and age.

At the end, the researchers put the final model inside a smartphone application. This application is pending approval of the US Food and Drug Administration to allow its use and circulation.

6.2 Medicine and Healthcare Applications

The Artificial Intelligence application that we have indicated is one of the «disease diagnosis» applications. It is one of the main tasks in the field of medicine. Those tasks can be divided into three sections:

- Diagnosis
- Treatment
- Anticipation for prevention

In each of the three tasks, building blocks of Artificial Intelligence are used to form the required Artificial Intelligence system. As we said, if a specialist doctor wants to diagnose a patient's condition, they can use some tools that help them determine the type of disease and its severity like:

- Medical tests
- X-rays (or any similar resources, such as skin photos, the sound of a patient's cough, etc.)
- Previous medical reports of the same patient

If we want to build an Artificial Intelligence system that helps diagnose the patient's condition, we need the following building blocks to build an integrated model that works to give the correct diagnosis:

- Classification model that deals with test data
- Computer vision model for processing and analyzing X-rays (or cough sound recognition model)
- Natural Language Processing model to analyze previous medical reports and extract the most important points thereof

These three models (building blocks) are combined together in one integrated structure to form a diagnostic model. Of course, each disease has its own model. Such a model is trained on previous data of patients with the same disease.

Figure 6.1: Link to MIT News about the prediction of future breast cancer

Professor Regina Barzilay, a scientist specializing in Artificial Intelligence, was diagnosed with breast cancer in 2014. She began reviewing her previous X-rays before being diagnosed with cancer and compared them with the recent X-rays. She found that there were some spots in the old X-rays that doctors did not notice at that time. In the most recent X-rays, these spots had turned to tumors, on the basis of which she was diagnosed with the disease.

As a result, Barzilay developed an Artificial Intelligence model to detect these spots early to avoid the disease's progression to the extent where it would be difficult to treat. However, she was not satisfied only with X-rays, so she also used the building blocks we mentioned to form the integrated model that combines X-rays, patient medical history, family medical history, information of the previous biopsy taken from the patient, patient's age and race, etc.

The model developed by Barzilay was able to detect cancer at an early stage, with an accuracy of 97% instead of the 79% that was previously achieved.

6.3 Recommender Systems

Do you watch Netflix or listen to Spotify? Do you like what the two platforms recommend to you once you're done watching an episode or listening to a song? Do you feel that both platforms have understood and realized what your favorite movies or songs are, or what your taste is?

This is what we call «Recommender Systems» or «Recommenders,» which are Artificial Intelligence systems that are able to determine the best «things» that they may «recommend» to the user. This category of systems and applications include what you find on e-shopping sites and applications. Each user will see their own version of the website's pages. This is because they will see a group of products that may seem suitable for them more than other users!

These systems use the Artificial Intelligence technology or models called «Generative Models». These models:

1. Analyze historical data and find the preferences of the user (ex: movies, songs, or products)
2. Try to initially classify the current user. Then, the user's class is modified according to their future behavior (for example, viewing or purchasing new products)
3. Generate a preferences list for this user based on the two previous steps

You can imagine other applications of the recommender systems in every field, whether it is entertainment or another sensitive field such as health care. Treatment methods that suit some patients may not suit others, so recommender systems may find the best methods that suit the patient and help increase the likelihood of their recovery by using steps similar to what we have mentioned above.

6.4 GANGogh

GANs or «Generative Adversarial Networks» is the name of deep neural networks that are used in image processing. «GANGogh» is not a typographical error, but a project whose name is inspired by the name of the famous painter «Van Gogh» mashed with the name GAN. This project resulted in the so-called «Style Transfer» technique. This means that if Artificial Intelligence techniques for «data regeneration» can generate a list of preferences for a new e-shopper, why don't we use the same technology to regenerate more complex things like images and paintings?

Figure 6.2: Link to GANGogh project.

In the GANGogh project, this technique was used, after applying some modifications, to recreate paintings that had not been painted before as if we were actually in front of an actual Van Gogh or Picasso painting. «While we do not believe that our model 'solves' the problem of art generation, we hope to have offered insights into the ways in which GANs can be used to generate novel art....», the two students who carried out the project said. The matter is not over yet.

6.5 Artificial Intelligence Ethics

In our review of the previous applications, we tried to go deeper than what you could read in the news about similar applications so that you can, in your organization or company, think of realistic applications that use Artificial Intelligence. The list is long.

At the moment, it is difficult, perhaps impossible, to find a scientist or researcher familiar with the different applications of Artificial Intelligence in various fields. The common, important point between various fields is the ethical effects of Artificial Intelligence. We will give two simple examples to shed light on this challenge, which needs more comprehensive discussions to cover it.

Let us assume that a university in Africa developed a model to identify people with COVID-19 by photographing them while entering airports. As this model has proved its effectiveness and achieved high accuracy in identifying infected people, a European country decided to buy and use it. What do we expect the result to be?

This model or application and its creators will be accused of «discrimination» because it will only be able to identify patients of «African» race. The fact is that the Artificial Intelligence system that we have so far, as we explained in chapter 1, is not real intelligence but rather an equation that approximates new data results based on the data it has been trained on. If the nature of the new data differs from the training data, the «Artificial Intelligence» would fail to be intelligent.

In the African university, the model was trained on images of infected and healthy «Africans», who are the least common race in the European country. Therefore, the result of deploying the model in a different environment will inevitably be a failure in comparison to the impressive success it achieved in its original environment. In other cases, the failure of the AI model could stay hidden to those operating it and unfairly cause problems to many people. Every Artificial Intelligence system depends on its training data, which, in turn, represents the environment from which it was taken. It also depends on the method in which the data was collected!

The second example concerns some life or health insurance companies that want to make their monthly «insurance policy» vary depending on the behavior of each person and how much they stay fit. The insurance company may give you the option to allow their Artificial Intelligence applications to communicate with the vital signs reader (like the Apple Watch) that you wear on your hand. So, if you, for example, exercise this month, what you will pay next month will be less. The company might also use some prediction model to know when they should terminate your contract!

Artificial Intelligence opens new horizons to people and organizations. However, it also creates new and unexpected ethical challenges. Thus, it is every organization's responsibility to set frameworks to regulate the work of its Artificial Intelligence teams.

CHAPTER 7

QUANTUM COMPUTING

If you lived in the 1970s, you would be familiar with the old TVs which used vacuum tubes that needed some time for their valves to reach the appropriate temperature in order to give a clear image. This type of TV disappeared after the widespread use of «transistors» or «semiconductors» in televisions. The invention of the transistor was a great leap in technology. It was a real paradigm shift and was the main reason of the facilitation of the manufacture of computers in various shapes and sizes.

The shift that we are currently looking at, upon the launch of the first commercial quantum computer, may be greater than the one which occurred when the transistor was invented. It will be a new era when these computers will be able to solve problems that are impossible to solve by traditional computers. They will take just minutes or hours to solve some problems that were once estimated to take hundreds of years.

Before we talk about quantum computing, it is worth reviewing some basics first.

7.1 Quantum Physics

In 1900, while trying to explain the phenomenon of radiation from black objects upon heating, the German physicist, Max Planck, developed the theory of quantum physics, as «classical» physics had failed to explain this phenomenon as well as other natural phenomena. Quantum theory was, along with other theories formulated by contemporary scientists such as Albert Einstein, the base on which so-called «modern physics» was built.

Figure 7.1: A Quantum Computer.

Quantum theory was called such because it cites that when energy is emitted from a particle, it is not emitted continuously, but in the form of quanta (plural of quantum), which is the smallest quantity a particle can emit. In fact, quantum physics came to explain natural phenomena at the atomic level when classical physics had failed to do so.

Now, we can focus on the scientific basis of quantum computers. In quantum physics, a particle has a dual nature, that is, a particle such as an «electron» behaves like an object that has a mass and also as a wave that moves in space. The waves intersect and overlap, which is the scientific basis for the «superposition» property which will be mentioned later. This level of detail should suffice for the scope of this book.

7.2 Computing

Computing is a machine's ability to perform arithmetic and logical operations, which are the main function of the Central Processing Unit (CPU) that most of us know. Arithmetic operations are addition, subtraction, multiplication, and division, of numbers and fractions, no matter how large or small their value is. Logical operations are more like conditional operations; for instance, «If we got an apple or orange, we got a fruit,» meaning that the goal is achieved by achieving one of the two conditions. This is what's called a «logical OR operation». AND, XOR, and others are also logical operations whcih are beyond the scope of this book.

The idea, on which the computer was built, is to convert all required functions into arithmetic or logical operations, which happens by storing all types of data in a numerical format, i.e. numbers. The Central Processing Unit can then perform arithmetic and logical operations on those numbers to produce outputs. These outputs are stored in the memory or restored to their original format (a photo for example) before they are displayed on the screen.

Let's say you want to modify a photo. You will scan and save it as a «digital» file on your computer, then use a photoshop application to modify it. What photoshop does when you do any modification to the image is to send previously-programmed commands to the Central Processing Unit, which turns them into arithmetic and logical operations that the processor performs on the image data, and the result of these operations is the modified image.

When a processor has a speed of 3 GHz, for example, it means the processor is able to perform nearly half a billion instructions per second. Central Processing Units performs these operations sequentially, while Graphics Processing Units (GPUs) can do parallel arithmetic operations. This capability gives GPUs a great advantage over CPUs in image and video processing software, as well as Artificial Intelligence software.

7.3 Algorithms

As mentioned earlier in the book, algorithms are well-defined instructions that perform a specific task or function. In theory, it is possible to write an algorithm for anything. The "recipe" for making a birthday cake is a simple algorithm, while the "recipe" for how Google searches for a word you entered in the search box is a very complex one.

Algorithms have degrees of complexity that can be measured in specific ways developed by scientists. The degree of complexity reflects the amount of computing and the length of time required by the algorithm to obtain the results (for example: the power and speed of the computer and the time which Google's algorithm would need to obtain search results).

As indicated earlier, the emergence of more effective algorithms and the introduction of improvements to existing ones were among the main reasons for the boom in the field of Artificial Intelligence, in addition to the emergence of computers with super-capabilities. This means that the more computers are able to implement more complex algorithms, the more we can achieve in various scientific and applied fields.

In every field, there are theories that have not gone beyond theory to practical applications because, when converted into algorithms, they are excessively complex ones which available computing capabilities cannot afford. Such complex algorithm may require tens or hundreds of years to finish.

7.4 What is Quantum Computing?

Quantum computing involves the use of special processors whose design is based on the principles of quantum physics and mechanics. The design grants higher computing performance than the most powerful state-of-the-art classical computers by hundreds or thousands of times. Classical computers use «bits», which are a binary storage unit. One «bit» can store either a one or a zero. Meanwhile; quantum computers use «qubits,» which are characterized by two main features that give the quantum computer its superiority:

7.4.1 Superposition

The **«qubit»** can also store a one or a zero, however it has a magic-like feature, that is its ability to store a one and a zero simultaneously in what is called the superposition phenomenon. It is one of the most important phenomena that were brought about by quantum physics.

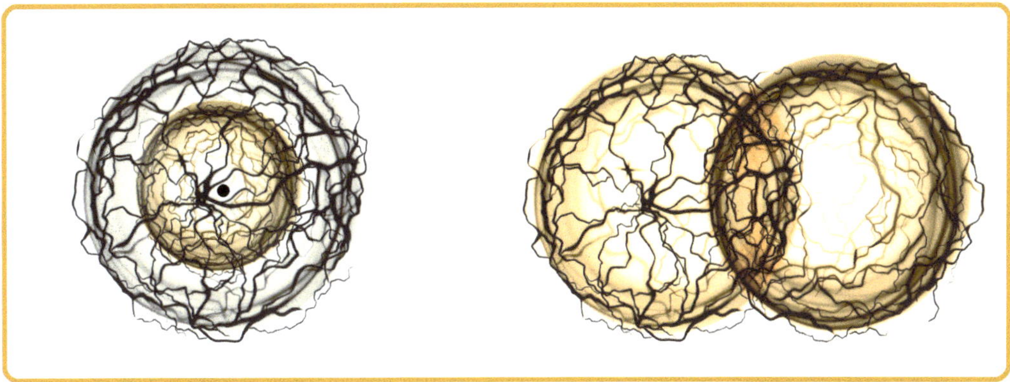

Figure 7.1: When superposition occurs, the atom or particle can be in two states at the same time (left) or in two places at the same time (right)

Instead of trying to understand superposition, it is better to try to understand its effect on the field of quantum computing; for example, if we use 4 «bits,» they can only store a single number with a value between 0-15, while the use of 4 «qubits» grants us the ability to store all the 16 numbers in the range 0-15, which is equivalent to 2^4. And so if the number of qubits is increased to 64, then we will reach 18,446,744,073,709,600,000 numbers instead of 16, and a quantum computer, which uses 300 qubits, could represent values that exceed the number of atoms existing in our visible universe.

7.4.1 Quantum Entanglement

Quantum Entanglement is one of the characteristics that Einstein discovered and described as «spooky action at a distance.» It allows two particles to affect each other's behavior instantly across vast distances. For example, if one of them is in China and the other in Morocco, the moment the state of one of them is changed, the state of the other one would change too, regardless of the distance betweem them.

Therefore, if two qubits are entangled, it is possible to know the state of both of them by observing the state of one. This property is used in cybersecurity applications, as we will explain later. Moreover, our ability to change the state of all entangled qubits by changing the state of only one is the reason for the superiority of the quantum computer over its classical counterpart. Because instead of processing a group of numbers sequentially, as is the case in classical computing, we can process all numbers at the same time by entangling the qubits storing these numbers.

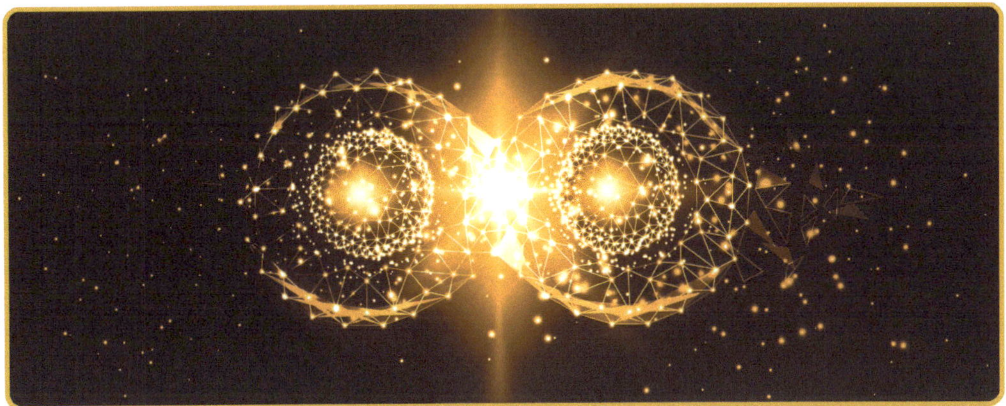

Figure 7.2: An artistic image of Quantum Entanglement between two particles

7.5. Quantum Computing Challenges

Some companies have made quantum computers available for commercial use only in the form of «cloud services,» led by IBM, Google, and Microsoft. D-Wave, a leading British company in the field of quantum computing, sells a special-purpose quantum computer. These companies, along with other major technology companies, have been making huge investments in quantum technology research. The most prestigious of universities all over the world also participate in these efforts because the challenges that impede reaching quantum supremacy are multiple and complex due to their origination from quantum physics. Accordingly, most scientists estimate it will be a decade until companies can universally manufacture a full-functional (universal) quantum computer.

7.5.1 Quantum Supremacy

Quantum Supremacy means that a quantum computer has reached a point where it outperforms all classical computers in the world; that is, it can solve problems that supercomputers have been unable to solve at all or in a reasonable time frame. To reach this point, researchers in Google declared at the end of 2019 that they had achieved this historical achievement, that their quantum computer which contains 54 qubits was able to actually perform calculations that today's classical computers can not. They also cited that their new Sycamore quantum computer could perform in 200 seconds a task that would take a conventional (classical) computer about 10,000 years.

In March 2020, Honeywell announced that it was able to develop a quantum computer that was more powerful than any other computer available in the market; this quantum computer contained 64 qubits. In June of the same year, the company actually revealed that its quantum computer had become available for service and used by some large corporations in the USA, such as JPMorgan Bank. The Honeywell quantum computer performed extremely complex math operations for JPMorgan, which could not be performed by conventional computers.

It's clear now that the main challenge is to manufacture a quantum computer that contains a large number of qubits that can work together. So why is it so difficult to achieve this?

7.5.2 Manufacturing Qubits

The main element in a quantum computer is the qubit, specifically the unique superposition state of qubits. However, this state is still unstable and cannot be preserved while performing arithmetic operations, as some types of qubits need to exist at absolute zero (-273.15° C) in order to maintain the superposition state as long as possible.

In addition, creating entanglement between qubits is very difficult. In fact, numbers like 54 qubits and 64 qubits, which were reached by Google and Honeywell, are incredible achievements. A regular computer may contain a memory of 16 billion bits (16 GB RAM); however, a quantum computer with such a small number of qubits is still outperforming the most powerful classical computer that exist today due to the superposition state characteristics mentioned above.

7.5.3 Teleportation

In order for the «quantum» work system to be complete, there must be a quantum internet that connects the quantum computers and transmits qubits between them. As we mentioned earlier, the basis for «teleportation» is the «quantum entanglement» feature, but quantum entanglement in general is still theoretical. As for its practical reality, it is still limited by the distance between the two entangled particles. The ultimate result reached by scientists was made by a team of Chinese scientists in February 2020, who maintained the entanglement betwee n two objects standing and effective up to a distance of 50 kilometers. An American team working in one of the US Department of Energy projects was able to reach a distance of 18 kilometers.

Figure 7.2: In 2019, Google announced its quantum computer that achieved, for the first time, «quantum supremacy»

CHAPTER 8

APPLICATIONS OF QUANTUM COMPUTING

The following table shows multiple potential use cases for Quantum Computing technologies across different sectors. In this chapter, we will focus on the most mature use cases; that is, they have either already been implemented or the research around them has at leas reached a very advanced state.

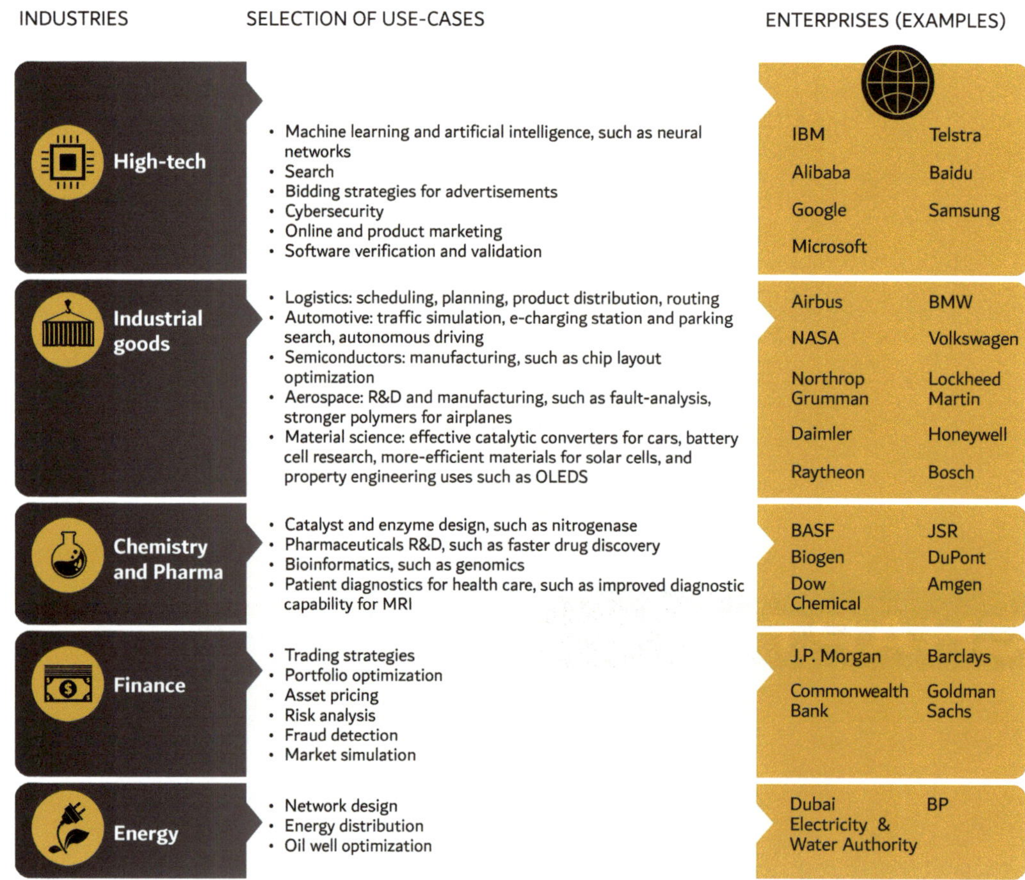

INDUSTRIES	SELECTION OF USE-CASES	ENTERPRISES (EXAMPLES)
High-tech	• Machine learning and artificial intelligence, such as neural networks • Search • Bidding strategies for advertisements • Cybersecurity • Online and product marketing • Software verification and validation	IBM, Telstra, Alibaba, Baidu, Google, Samsung, Microsoft
Industrial goods	• Logistics: scheduling, planning, product distribution, routing • Automotive: traffic simulation, e-charging station and parking search, autonomous driving • Semiconductors: manufacturing, such as chip layout optimization • Aerospace: R&D and manufacturing, such as fault-analysis, stronger polymers for airplanes • Material science: effective catalytic converters for cars, battery cell research, more-efficient materials for solar cells, and property engineering uses such as OLEDS	Airbus, BMW, NASA, Volkswagen, Northrop Grumman, Lockheed Martin, Daimler, Honeywell, Raytheon, Bosch
Chemistry and Pharma	• Catalyst and enzyme design, such as nitrogenase • Pharmaceuticals R&D, such as faster drug discovery • Bioinformatics, such as genomics • Patient diagnostics for health care, such as improved diagnostic capability for MRI	BASF, JSR, Biogen, DuPont, Dow Chemical, Amgen
Finance	• Trading strategies • Portfolio optimization • Asset pricing • Risk analysis • Fraud detection • Market simulation	J.P. Morgan, Barclays, Commonwealth Bank, Goldman Sachs
Energy	• Network design • Energy distribution • Oil well optimization	Dubai Electricity & Water Authority, BP

Source: BCG analysis.

Before we may go into detail let us answer a simple question: is a quantum computer faster than a classical computer? No, but the real difference is its ability to process data in parallel, or, in other words, «processing data in real time,» which means that the efficiency of a quantum computer depends on the nature of the problem it is addressing. There are problems in which a quantum computer may be slower than its classical counterpart, and while other issues are possible in theory, a classical computer may take hundreds of years to process them while a quantum computer can process them in several hours.

8.1 Cybersecurity

Quantum computing has two main applications in cybersecurity. The first is related to data encryption, and the second is to secure data when transferred , in relation to the security of the Internet and networks.

8.1.1 Quantum Cryptographic Algorithms

The first application uses advanced algorithms which are made practically possible by a quantum computer. Peter Shor, professor at Massachusetts Institute of Technology and one of the pioneers of quantum computing, developed an algorithm for factoring numbers using quantum computing. As currently known, factorization is the main technique in data encoding processes due to the difficulty to decode it. Shor's algorithm, when applied, will reduce the time needed to factorize a number exponentially. To be more specific, a regular algorithm for factoring a number consisting of 15 digits needs 32,768 steps, and by using Shor's algorithm, it will need 3,375 steps, and even more so, if the number consists of 20 digits, we will need 1,048,576 steps in comparison to the 800 steps of Shor's algorithm.

Unfortunately, this means that many cryptographic systems currently in place will be easy to crack in hours but also that new systems and technologies will appear to save data. Shor's algorithm alone poses a threat to public-key cryptographic systems such as RSA, which are used frequently in our daily activities when surfing the Internet and whose mathematical defenses depend in part on how difficult it is to perform the opposite steps to derive the results of multiplying very large primes together. In fact, report on quantum computing that was published in 2018 by the US National Academies of Sciences, Engineering, and Medicine predicted that a high-capacity quantum computer implementing Shor's algorithm would be able to crack the executive version of RSA algorithm with a 1,024-bit key in less than one day.

8.1.2 Quantum teleportation

The second application in the field of cybersecurity depends on entanglement. Qubits cannot be copied like the bits we are currently using, because when trying to read the value of a qubit, it changes. This means that if someone wants to eavesdrop on a connection between two other parties, they will be detected as soon as they attempt reading the first transferred qubit.

To transfer data between two parties, it is enough to have a pair of entangled qubits, where one of them is kept on the sender's device and the other can be transferred to the receiver's device, because then every change to one of the qubits will be reflected immediately on the other qubit, as if we created a gap in time and space between the two ends, that is until one of the qubits is observed. So there is no communication channel to be hacked here.

Although the method of data transfer using qubits is theoretically impossible to hack, it is still like anything else when applied—there will be several loop holes. Recently, a team from Jiao Tong University in Shanghai, China, cited that they found one of these forgotten vulnerabilities. Thanks to this discovery, the team was able to hack quantum cryptography with a high success rate, causing panic.

Instead of the team trying to read the qubits while being transported, which would have been a failure, they attacked the qubits when they were launched from the transmitter, which relies on the use of lasers to fire photons (the qubits) and on the change of frequency of the launched laser beam. This loophole gave them the power to control the qubits without the knowledge of the sender or the receiver.

8.1.3 Will quantum computers be able to hack cryptographic defenses soon?[12]

This is highly unlikely, as the US National Academies declared that quantum machines will need much higher processing capabilities than what today's best quantum ma-

[12] From an article published in MIT Technology Review

chines have achieved in order to pose a real threat. However, what some security researchers like to call «Y2Q» , the year when quantum computing cryptography cracking will become a big problem, could be arriving surprisingly fast. In 2015, researchers concluded that a quantum computer would need one billion qubits to crack an RSA system with a 2,048-bit key with great ease. One of the more recent works suggests that a computer using 20 million qubits could perform the task in just eight hours.

This still far exceeds the capabilities of today's most capable quantum machine, which uses 128 qubits. The advances being made in quantum computing, however,, remain unpredictable. Any company or government planning to store data for the coming decades should now think about the risks that this new technology poses, because the cryptography used to protect the data may be compromised at a later time.

However, it could take many years to re-encode massive amounts of historical data again using more robust defenses and so accordingly, it would be better to implement this now. This threat truly shines the light on the importance of a major push for the development of post-quantum cryptography.

8.1.4 Post-Quantum Cryptography (PQC)

PQC is the development of new types of cryptography methods which can be executed by conventional computers today but be immune to attacks that would be launched by quantum computers in the future. In 2016, the US National Institute of Standards and Technology launched a process to develop standards for post-quantum cryptography for government use. It was able to decrease the initial group of 69 proposals to just 26. However, it says the draft standards would likely not come into existence before 2022.

The pressure remains high because cryptography techniques are an integral part of many different systems. Therefore, dismantling them and implementing new technologies may take a very long time. In fact, the 2018 National Academies study indicated that it took more than a decade to completely abandon a widespread cryptographic method that turned out to be flawed. Given the speed at which quantum computing is evolving, the world may not have much time to confront this new security threat.

8.2 Artificial Intelligence and Machine Learning

Most Artificial Intelligence and Machine Learning algorithms rely on the principles of «linear algebra,» which is what quantum computing has mastered. Therefore, in most of the algorithms, if used with quantum computers, the time and computing power that they need will often diminish in an exponential fashion (for example: an algorithm requiring 1,000 steps will only require 3 steps) which leads to the ability to process even larger amounts of data and use applications that were not possible before.

The matter is not only related to the speed of the implementation of an algorithm, but also the way quantum computing works, which opens the door to developing algorithms of a different nature, as indicated by Dr. Maria Schuld.[13] In one of her lectures, she said, «The hope is that Quantum Machine Learning will achieve real Artificial Intelligence.» Therefore, investing in quantum algorithms may bear unexpected results that will help in the development of Artificial Intelligence itself and perhaps the achievement of General Artificial Intelligence that we mentioned at the beginning of the book.

As an example, in image processing applications, the «traditional» algorithms process image in a sequential manner; that is, they recognize the image part by part, but by using quantum algorithms, it may be possible to identify objects and people in the image simultaneously, which may help us avoid many of the errors that occur due to the sequential method.

8.3 Chemistry and Pharmaceutical Industry

Anika Chebrolu, a 14-year-old American girl of Indian origin, discovered the structure of a molecule that could distinguish and bind to the protein of the COVID-19 virus, which provided a basis for making drugs that could isolate and target the virus without harming the human body. What the clever girl did was use an algorithm that explored different chemical molecules and tested them with the target-

13 She is South African scientist. She has specialized in quantum machine learning research and established one of the most important open platforms for developing quantum machine learning algorithms (PennyLane.ai).

ed coronavirus protein, but this exploration process is usually expensive in terms of time and computation, and those who implement these types of alogrithms always try to optimize them through various improvements to shorten time and cost.

This is an example where quantum computing will have the upper hand and even turn a dream into reality. The ability to process data simultaneously, as explained above, will give the ability quantum computers to explore and test thousands or millions of possible combinations simultaneously instead of sequentially exploring and testing each possible combination.

There are many other examples, but they are all based on the same idea, which is the ability to process data simultaneously, including what Google did in August 2020, when it simulated a chemical reaction, giving scientists great hope to understand how chemical reactions actually happen.

8.4 How to Be Prepared for the Quantum Era?

Quantum computing research is divided into several main sections:

- **Quantum Computer Industry**

  This includes research on materials used in the qubit industry and advanced technologies used in creating quantum systems, such as putting those qubits at a temperature of absolute zero or using other technologies such as the «particle trap» which Honeywell used to create its quantum computer.

- **Operating Systems Development**

Quantum computers will differ in its structure from the traditional computer, just as the way it processes data is different. If we add to that its connection via the quantum internet, we need to design and build it its own Operating Systems.

- **Development of Quantum Algorithms**

Quantum Algorithms are included in all applications that we have indicated, with «Machine Learning.» as the top application. Quantum algorithm research currently relies on quantum computer simulation systems, since scientists do not want to wait until an effective quantum computer is available to complete their research. Rather, development of quantum algorithms has revealed new types of algorithms which may be used with traditional computers because they can sometimes outperform current algorithms.

- **Quantum Applications and Software**

These are applications directly used. We have already introduced some of them, but we are still at the beginning and it is expected that new applications in various fields are going to be introduced every month in the coming years.

8.4 How to Be Prepared for the Quantum Era?

In your organization, the department concerned with strategy and creativity should follow the four research sections mentioned above. For the first two sections, they are closer to companies and institutions specialized in technology, while all institutions and companies should keep track of the progress of the last two. As we indicated earlier, JPMorgan Bank, the largest bank in the United States, has already started using quantum computers.

Many of the leading companies in quantum computing create development platforms and environments that use classical simulators of quantum computers instead of the real thing. Then there are other companies who have even created programming languages and libraries for programming quantum computers, which naturally differ from classical programming in terms of rationale, principle, and method of implementation.

As we mentioned earlier, some cloud services companies have provided quantum computing services, even as just a beta form, as well as quantum computer simulation services. Therefore, major institutions and government agencies should take the initiative to profusely enter this field and invest in these services that are mostly free of charge. Because even if «tech news» do not focus enough on this technology, it does not mean that it is not important. Rather the principles of this technology will remain very difficult until they are packaged in shiny marketing templates, as they are still limited to the scientists and engineers circles.

From another, more important, point of view, it is not possible to predict the uses of quantum computing. Scientists are busier with the manufacturing of the quantum computer than with its uses, which are often decided by the market and the competition. Making quantum computers available for people will definitely create countless uses and applications.

It is worth mentioning here that in 1943, Thomas Watson, chairman of IBM, said, «I think there is a world market for maybe five computers.» Now, there are five in every household.

8.5 Quantum Technology Predictions for 2021

Let's try to explore the near future [14] of quantum computing and quantum technology in general. The company IQT Research prepared a report on its predictions for 2021 and focused on four main predictions that would govern progress in the field this year. A little more than a year ago, some serious technology journalists could have questioned whether or not quantum computers would be launched commercially, but now the debate revolves around how much a quantum computer can do and when. The debate has moved to the capabilities of the quantum computer when its actual existence used to be the focus of that debate.

Looking at what has been achieved in quantum technology in 2020, IQT Research believes that 2021 will be more than a special year. Here are four predictions for 2021:

---

[14] From an article by Mr. Lawrence Gasman, president of insidequantumtechnology.com

8.5 Quantum Technology Predictions for 2021

1. **Expected Explosive Growth of Cybersecurity Markets.**

   IQT Research predicts a rapid move in 2021 for quantum cybersecurity, with new products driven by (1) cyberattacks which are seen as an increasing threat to national security in a number of countries; and (2) concerns about weak cryptocurrencies in a world where Bitcoin could become the common way to exchange and store value. In fact, there is an emerging debate over whether Bitcoin needs to add a quantum security feature or whether its current scurity position is sufficient.

   Secure quantum phones by Samsung, possibly Huawei, and others will soon be the focal point of consumers as the way to ward off hackers and protect e-commerce on mobile devices. Meanwhile, secure quantum computing will also become the stated goal of startups and renamed products in cybersecurity companies everywhere.

2. **Popularity of Personal Quantum Computers in 2021.**

   IQT Research launched its prediction over a year ago that the «next big thing» in quantum computing was personal quantum computers. IonQ recently announced that we are only five years away from the debut of this computer. Chalmers University of Technology has already built a small quantum computer, although it was intended for specific experimental purposes.

   Currently, the personal quantum computer is definitely a controversial idea. However, IQT Research believes that it will become a common commodity by the end of 2021. A commercial quantum computer will not be available for several years; maybe longer than IonQ thinks. However, we certainly won't wait for decades, as it is likely that this will expand the quantum computer market in the same way that minicomputers were popular 60 years ago.

The personal quantum computer may represent a challenge to the cloud services currently prevalent in quantum computing and may also mean a change in the field of quantum technology. In fact, not all quantum computer technologies are suitable for miniaturization and usage in a personal or desk computer. In addition, this will affect the association of specific technologies with specific companies, as personal quantum computers will have a profound impact on market shares of each company in the future. Companies promoting «quantum microcomputers» may be the most attractive for investment. Nothing is certain here except that we will hear more about personal quantum computers - possibly under another name - in 2021.

3. **Increased Interest in Quantum Technology could Negatively Impact its Advancement.**

With the increase of competition between countries in quantum technology and confidence in existing research predictions in said area, it is anticipated that this will negatively affect the cooperation between universities and companies from different countries, especially with the increased focus on quantum cybersecurity applications.

The matter also has a positive impact, as the increase of competition between countries will provide increased funding from governments to universities to support research.

4. **Values of Quantitative Technology Companies**

   IQT Research expects that in 2021, quantum computers would grow exponentially in terms of number of qubits that are dealt with and the associated materials and equipment, leading to an increase in the threat that quantum computing poses to standard public-key cryptography systems. This will result in a boom in quantum secure technology. At the same time, quantum phones and the dreams of personal quantum computers will give rise to early evidence that there were companies built around the notion of a «mass market» for quantum technology.

All above explanations may describe the situation after a year. But where will the fund come to finance such an expansion in the field of quantum computing? Most likely, as we indicated, governments themselves will provide the necessary funding in light of the raging race to pioneer quantum computing technology.

What is still less clear is the market assessments of quantum computing companies which are progressively increasing. What Mr. Gasman expects, according to one of his sources, is that the market value of Rigetti is on its way to reach USD one billion, and even the Washington Post said that 2021 would be a big event for initial public offerings of quantum technology companies.

ANNEX A

COMPONENTS OF QUANTUM COMPUTER

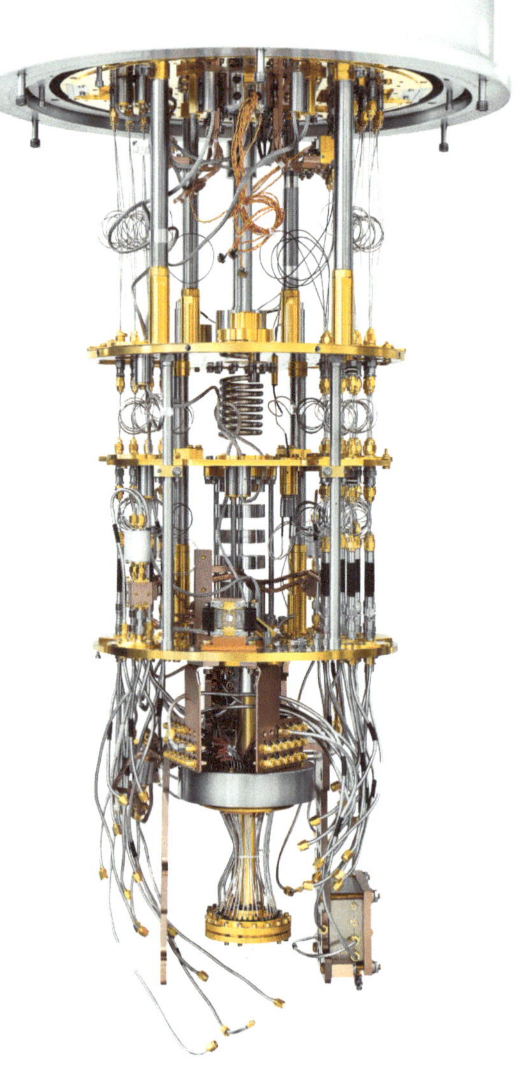

Rigetti[15] has developed various types of quantum computers to advance quantum computer research. It has promised to provide the best quantum computer and make it more accessible to its customers than other developers.

[15] According to Rigetti's website, a leading quantum computing company

9.1 Shell

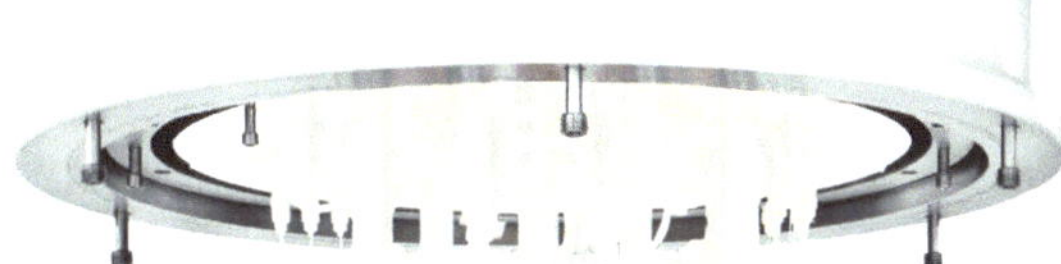

It consists of five «metal castings» like the upper silver part shown in the image, which nest inside each other, with all the computer components being kept in the last one.

The shell acts as a thermal insulating shield that envelops the quantum computer to maintain everything at absolute zero, or 273.15 Celsius and vacuum-sealed; two important characteristics of a quantum computer.

9.2 Nerves

Nerves are cables delivering signals to and from the master chip to control the qubits' operations and return the readings and results from those qubits to the master chip.

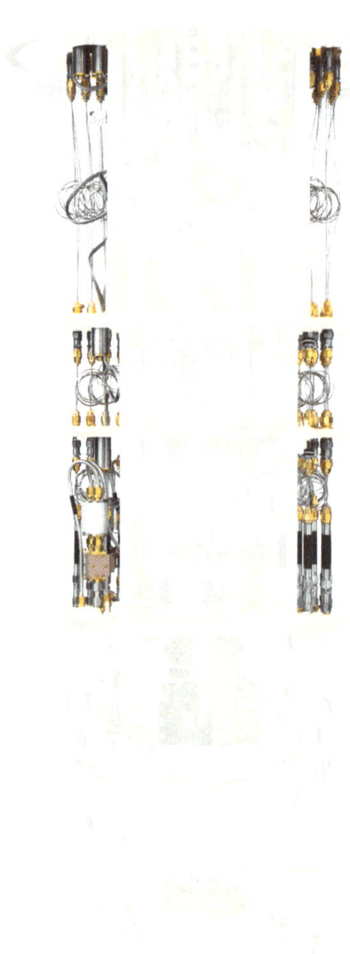

9.3 Skeleton

The skeleton is the golden plates separating cooling zones. At the bottom, they plunge to one hundredth of a Kelvin, which is hundreds of times as cold as outer space.

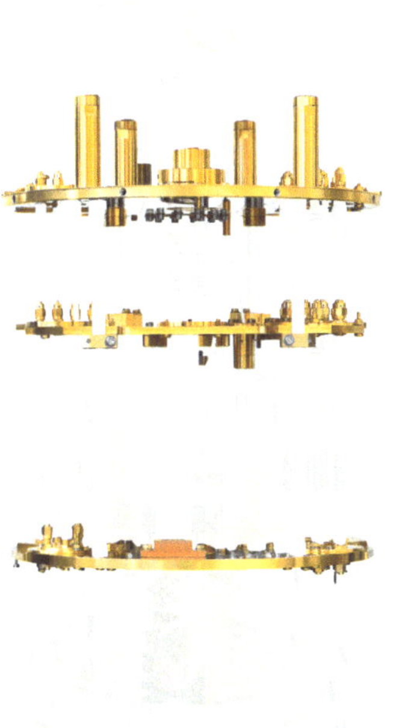

9.4 Heart

This is the inside of the device that is responsible for the cooling process, in which different forms of liquid helium, such as helium 3 and helium 4, separate and evaporate to absorb and diffuse the heat.

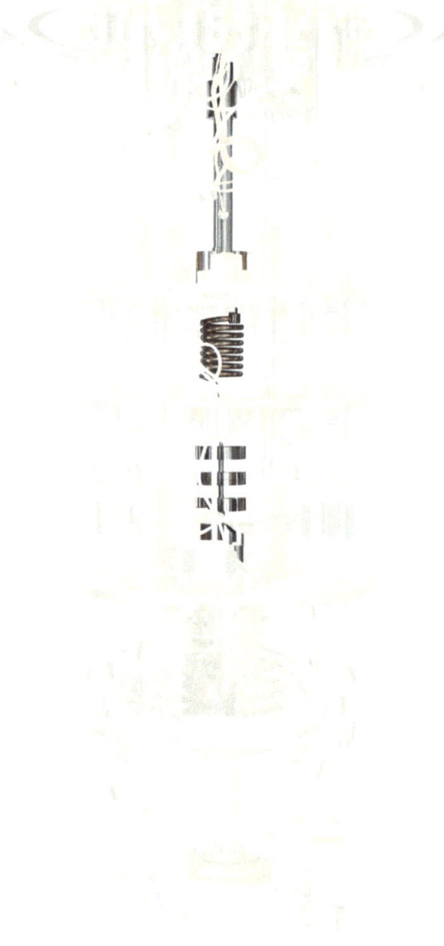

9.5 Brain

The QPU (Quantum Processing Unit) features a gold-plated copper disk with a silicon chip inside that contains the machine's brain.

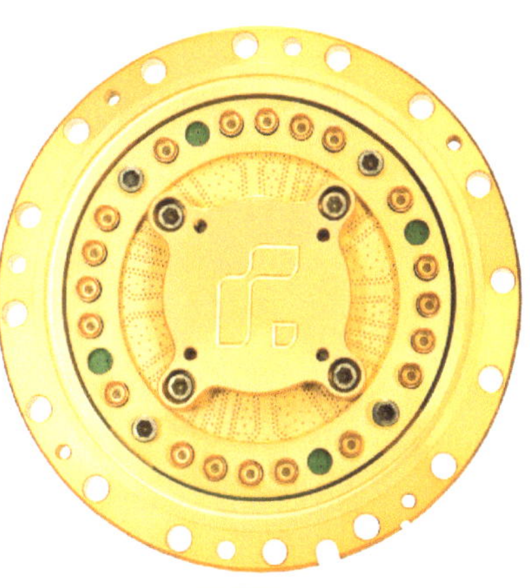

ANNEX B

QUANTUM COMPUTING BUSINESS MAP

10.1 Countries Investing in Quantum Computing

To be a leader in the field of quantum technology, China has aimed to be at the forefront of research. China launched the first quantum satellite in 2016, which was the subject of a research paper by an American Studies Center that sheds light on how «China is positioning itself as a central force in quantum science.»

To understand the strategic potential that quantum technology holds, the United States, Germany, Russia, India, and the European Union have intensified their efforts toward developing quantum computing. In the USA, former President Trump established the National Quantum Initiative Advisory Committee (NQIAC) in 2019 according to a specially enacted law that was signed in late 2018; this law authorizes the USA to spend $1.2 billion on quantum science over the next five years.

In its 2020 budget, the Indian government announced a national mission for quantum technologies and applications at a total cost of CR 8,000 ($1.12 billion) for five years, while Europe has a €1 billion initiative that provides funding for all quantum technology research and work over the next ten years.

In October 2019, the first quantum computer prototype was launched in Russia, while in Germany, Fraunhofer-Gesellschaft, Europe's leading organization for applied research, has partnered with IBM to conduct advanced research in quantum computing.

China Leads in Publications on Quantum Computing, but the US Is More Integrated Internationally

China leads by country
EMEA leads by region

Number of scientific publications since 2013

Country	Publications
China	2,986
USA	2,494
Germany	1,086
UK	947
Japan	635
Canada	589
Australia	487
Italy	464
France	453
India	406
Other countries	4,011

Number of scientific publications since 2013

Region	Publications
EMEA	**6,013**
Asia-Pacific	**5,891**
Americas	**3,600**

US has strongest institutional collaborations[1]

	China	US	Germany	UK	Japan	Canada	Australia	Italy	France	India
China	1,529									
USA	224	894								
Germany	102	240	309							
UK	116	288	187	248						
Japan	116	210	124	102	239					
Canada	194	187	82	70	35	221				
Australia	59	80	54	68	35	66	121			
Italy	25	64	124	135	14	26	22	271		
France	28	96	111	116	95	19	35	88	173	
India	10	19	20	6	7	10	7	1	7	156

Sources: Web of Science; BCG Center for Innovation Analytics.
Note: Analysis based on approximately 10,000 scientific publications related to quantum computing submitted from 2013 to mid-2018; EMEA=Europe, Middle East, Africa
[1]Where two or more universities from the same country were affiliated with the same publication, they were counted as one internal collaboration.

Quantum Computing Patents Are Increasing Quickly

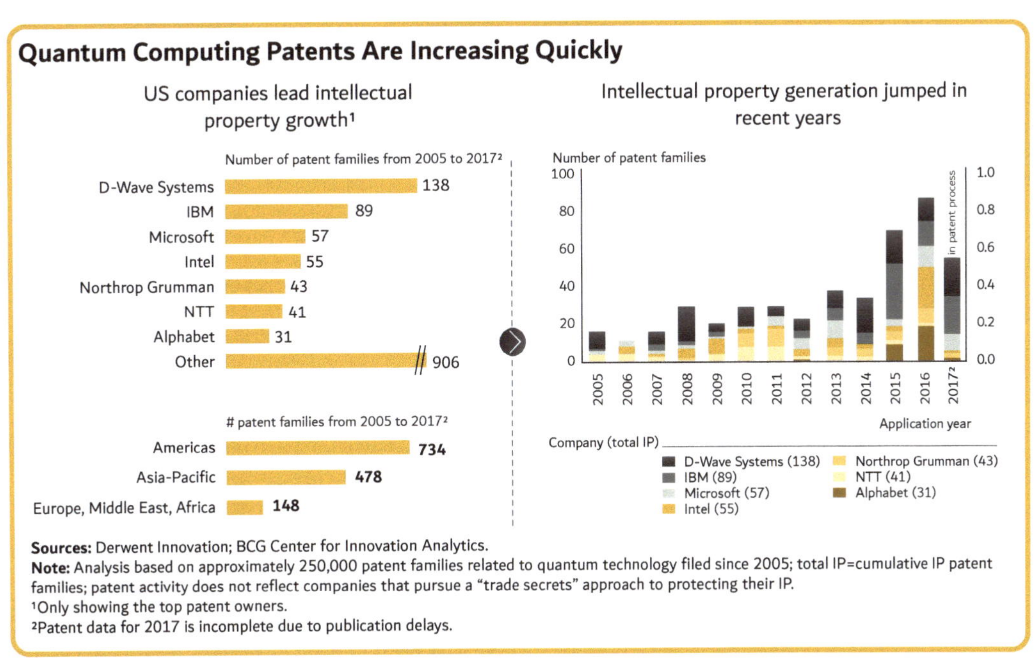

Sources: Derwent Innovation; BCG Center for Innovation Analytics.
Note: Analysis based on approximately 250,000 patent families related to quantum technology filed since 2005; total IP=cumulative IP patent families; patent activity does not reflect companies that pursue a "trade secrets" approach to protecting their IP.
[1]Only showing the top patent owners.
[2]Patent data for 2017 is incomplete due to publication delays.

The above diagrams show the analysis of research efforts worldwide. It is clear that China, as we mentioned above, leads those efforts. However, the USA is keeping its advanced position between all players, moreover, USA's collaboration approach will eventually make a real difference.

10.2 Leading Companies

IBM is one of the pioneers in quantum computing. In January 2019, IBM unveiled the IBM Q System One, which is the first global, integrated quantum computing system designed for scientific and commercial use. In September, it opened the IBM Quantum Computing Center in New York to expand quantum computing systems for commercial and research activity. Recently, it has also invested in Cambridge Quantum Computing, which is one of the first startups to become part of IBM's Q network in 2018.

In October 2019, Google released an ad claiming «quantum supremacy» and published the results of the quantum supremacy experiment in an article on the website "Nature" titled «Quantum Supremacy Using a Programmable Superconducting Processor.» The phrase «quantum supremacy» was coined by John Preskill in 2012, when he wrote that one way to achieve such «quantum supremacy» would be «to run an algorithm on a quantum computer which solves a problem with a super-polynomial speedup relative to classical computers.» However, IBM has opposed Google's claim to «quantum supremacy».

10.2 Leading Companies

The following diagram shows how different players are positioning themselves in the quantum technology stack:

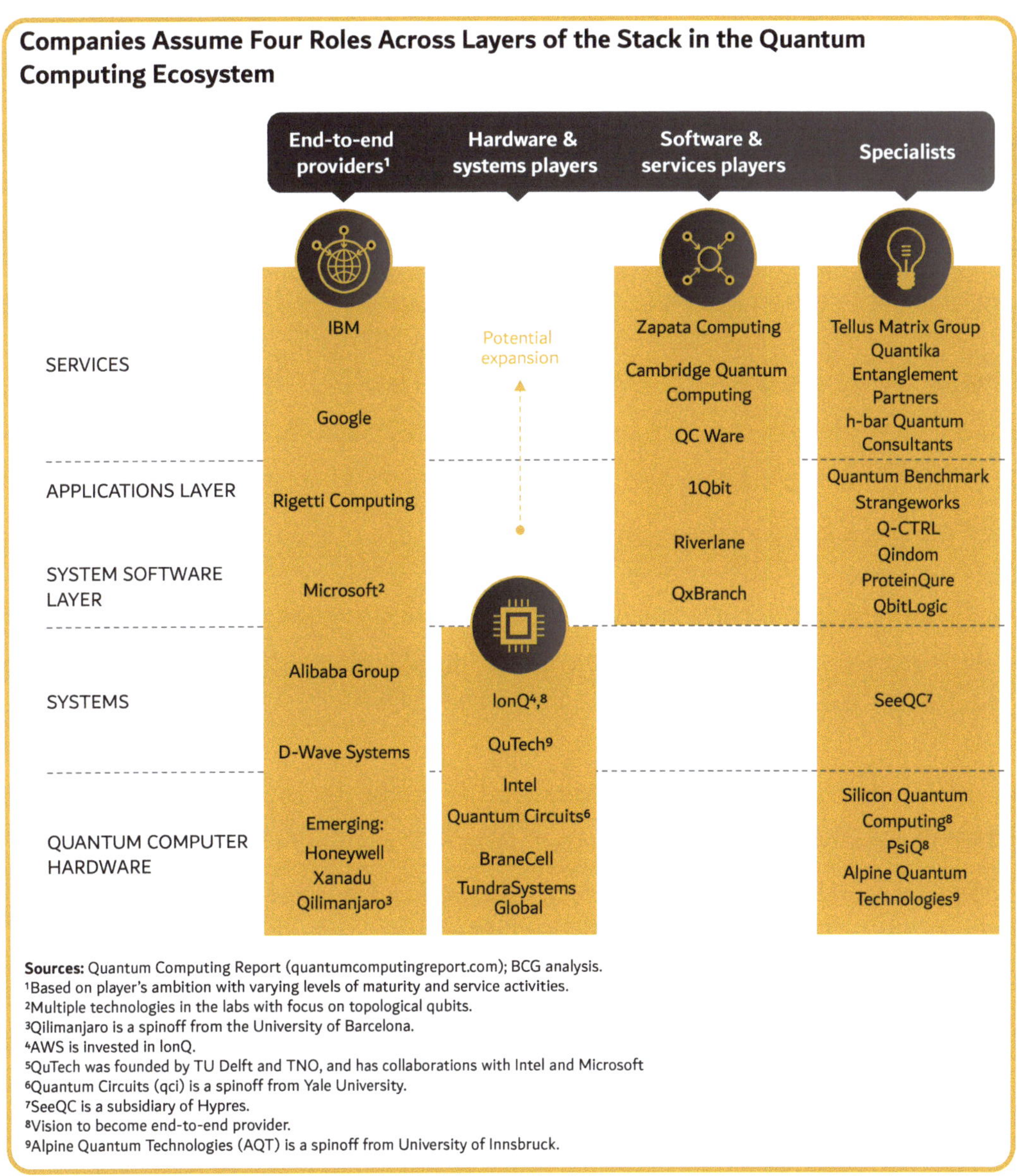

Sources: Quantum Computing Report (quantumcomputingreport.com); BCG analysis.
[1]Based on player's ambition with varying levels of maturity and service activities.
[2]Multiple technologies in the labs with focus on topological qubits.
[3]Qilimanjaro is a spinoff from the University of Barcelona.
[4]AWS is invested in IonQ.
[5]QuTech was founded by TU Delft and TNO, and has collaborations with Intel and Microsoft
[6]Quantum Circuits (qci) is a spinoff from Yale University.
[7]SeeQC is a subsidiary of Hypres.
[8]Vision to become end-to-end provider.
[9]Alpine Quantum Technologies (AQT) is a spinoff from University of Innsbruck.

Headquartered in Vancouver, Canada, D-Wave is the world's first commercial supplier of quantum computers, and its systems are used by organizations such as NEC, Volkswagen, DENSO, Lockheed Martin, USRA, USC, Los Alamos National Laboratory, and Oak Ridge National Laboratory. In February 2019, D-Wave announced an experimental model for its next-generation quantum computing platform that includes hardware, software, and other tools needed to accelerate and facilitate the delivery of quantum computing applications. In September 2019, it launched its next-generation quantum system called «Advantage,» which became available in the quantum cloud service called «Leap» at the end of 2020.

Amazon introduced the Amazon Braket service in late 2019 which was designed to allow its users to get some hands-on experience with qubits and quantum circuits. This service allows building and testing circuits in a simulated environment and then running them on a real quantum computer.

At the same time, Intel unveiled its first-of-its-kind cryogenic control chip - dubbed «Horse Ridge» - that could accelerate the development of integrated quantum computing systems.

Furthermore, companies such as Microsoft, Alibaba, Tencent, Nokia, Airbus, HP, AT&T Toshiba, Mitsubishi, SK Telecom, Raytheon, Lockheed Martin, Rigetti, Biogen, Volkswagen, and Amgen are conducting research and working on quantum computing applications.[16]

In China, which has become the leading country in quantum computing, Alibaba has launched a research laboratory focused on quantum computing. Likewise, Baidu,

---

16 Source: Nasdaq.com

the Chinese Artificial Intelligence giant, has established its own quantum computing institute in 2019 with the aim of making it one of the most important specialized research centers in the world.

10.3 Investment in Quantum Companies

Here are some of the most important emerging companies in quantum computing, the volume of investments in each of them, and the date of the last funding round:

Funding for Startups Has Increased in Recent Years

Startup	Total [US$ millions]	Most recent funding	Establishment
D-Wave Systems	**216.2**	December 2019	Canada - 1999
Rigetti Computing	**198.5**	August 2020	USA - 2013
PsiQ	**508.6**	April 2020	USA - 2016
Zapata Computing	**76.4**	November 202	USA - 2017
Cambridge Quantum Computing	**72.8**	December 2020	UK - 2014
1QBit	**35**	November 2017	Canada - 2012
lonQ	**82**	July 2020	USA - 2015
Xanadu	**35.6**	January 2020	Canada - 2016
IQM Quantum Computers	**84.3**	November 2020	Finland - 2018
Riverlane	**4.5**	June 2019	UK - 2017
Quantum Exchange	**23.5**	June 2018	USA - 2018
Quantum Computing	**4.3**	September 2020	USA - 2018

Sources: Crunchbase

10.4 The Most Important Quantum Programming Platforms

Microsoft launched its quantum computing platform in 2017. It supported the platform with a programming language for quantum software and called it Q#, similar to Microsoft's famous language C#. At the time this book was written, Microsoft does not have a quantum computer but instead relies on quantum computer simulation systems. It also provides services to run programs on true quantum computers through its partners, such as IonQ.

There are many software packages and libraries that aim to support programmers and facilitate the development of quantum applications without deeply understanding how quantum computers work, the most important of which are as follows:

Name of Library	Company	Work Environment
Ocean	D-Wave	Real computer
Qiskit	IBM	Real computer
Forest	Rigetti	Real computer
t|ket>	Cambridge Quantum Computing	Real computer
Quantum Development Kit	Microsoft	Simulator
Cirq	Google	Simulator
Strawberry Fields	Xanadu	Simulator

Table 10.1: Quantum Computing Platforms and Libraries

10.4 The Most Important Quantum Programming Platforms

It is worth noting that one of the most important platforms that appeared recently is Pennylane.ai, which works with most already existing available libraries, and can work with real quantum computers or simulation environments that they provide.

CONCLUSION

11.1 What was Missed in This Book?

Our goal for this book was to foresee the future of organizations in light of the changes and impacts caused by new technology on the business of these organizations and human life in general. Simultaneously, we wanted to use comprehensive language so that a non-specialized reader could gain the minimal knowledge about the fundamentals of the different technologies mentioned in this book.

Because of the limitations that we have set to keep the book easy and smooth for all readers, including maintaining a reasonable length to encourage the reader to read it completely in a few sittings, we did not cover all aspects of the topics mentioned in this book. So, what might be those aspects that we could have covered in a larger, more tech-savvy book?

11.1.1 Data Security

In the first few chapters of this book, we elaborated on the topic of Data, its importance to humans, and how Data is the true asset behind any digital system, especially Artificial Intelligence systems. However, we did not discuss much about how to protect and secure that data during its preservation or when processing it, and how this affects the different stages of an organization's data maturity. Data

Security is a major topic that all stakeholders in different organizations, especially decision-makers, should pay close attention to. It is increasingly important in the modern world, as everybody is moving to cloud solutions and services.

In the cloud, it is possible that an organization's data could exist outside the physical boundaries of the organization, or perhaps even outside the organization's country of operations.

Above all else, data security professionals often start with this question: You protect what against whom? Or, in other words: Do the cloud service providers guarantee the security of your hosted data, and if they do, can you trust the cloud service providers themselves?

11.1.2 Data Science and Artificial Intelligence

Data science and Artificial Intelligence are broad and complex fields that require dozens of books to explore their depths. We focused heavily on the topic of «Machine Learning» in our book because it is the hot AI topic and its applications are the most widespread among technology companies, organizations, and even scientists. If there was room, we would have explored the topics of Data Analytics and Data Visualization.

Data Analytics, which might appear like a less complex topic, provides great benefits to any organization. Additionally, an organization can gain these benefits in an easier and less expensive manner compared to what a «Machine Learning» system could cost. It also comes earlier in the data maturity path, before an organization can best utilize the «Machine Learning» techniques.

Data Visualization is another important topic, and it is the basis of what is currently known as «Info Graphics». Data Visualization, if it is effectively used by the IT team, can be the technology «translator» between the IT team and the rest of the organization's departments. It increasingly impacts how decision-makers can use an organization's big data in their decisions. Moreover, it is a powerful tool in the hands of marketing departments, as well as corporate relations and public affairs departments, to present information, products, and goals to the public.

While many scientists, as well as users, put a lot of hope on «Deep Learning» topics to advance Artificial Intelligence, there are other topics such as «Symbolic Artificial Intelligence» that we believe could become a game changer in the near future.

11.1.3 IT and Data Governance

It is not possible for digital transformation in any organization to succeed unless there is an IT governance framework in place, which is overseen by the data governance framework. The absence of these frameworks allows for any digital transformation initiative to begin, but not have it end. Governing the implementation of systems is mandatory to fulfill the functional requirements, while data governance is critical to prevent data leaks and to best utilize the Big Data of an organization.

We recommend reviewing one of the new frameworks, which may not have gained great popularity yet, but goes beyond the governance domain and to an end-to-end solution that manages all the affairs of information technology departments within the organization. This framework is called IT4IT and was built by The Open Group .It is known for developing standards and frameworks in the IT field that are not affiliated with any specific vendor.

11.1.4 Deeper in Quantum Computing

As we mentioned earlier, the foundation of quantum computing is quantum physics, which makes it the most difficult topic to go into. Given our limited space and the complexity of the topic, we believe we have done well introducing it.

However, the reader may wish to learn more about this interesting topic from other sources. In this book, we didn't cover all the different types of qubits and how to manufacture them, nor how this might affect the trends and speed of manufacturing the universal quantum computer.

The computer whose parts we presented in Appendix A is the most popular type among others that may outperform the normal computer in the near future, hence why we chose to include it.

We also did not mention one of the most important features of qubits, which is quantum interference. We also did not detail the Error Correction topic, which is the biggest obstacle to reaching the point where the universal quantum computer can be relied upon in all quantum computing applications.

At this point, we recommend the reader review in detail the main types of quantum computing from other sources, namely: Quantum Optimization, including «Quantum Annealing», and Quantum Simulation.

11.2 Conclusion

In the end, we hope that we were able to encourage you to pay more attention to the future of technology and how it might impact you as an individual as well as the organization that you may work for. If so, it would mean that we succeeded in pushing you to lay a plan to learn and read more about our selected topics in order to utilize them in your day-to-day activities.

We wanted this book to be a simple and easy-to-follow recipe for anyone who wanted to effectively use technology in their job. Accordingly, the middle of the book was a simple explanation of the idea of digital transformation, its importance, and how to develop a roadmap to achieve it. At the beginning of the book , we tried to merge the philosophy of data and its impact on our lives, and the history of technology in general, and Artificial Intelligence in particular. Our approach was to begin by presenting the raw materials that then became inputs to the digital transformation process so that the result is the smart enterprise, the Future Enterprise.

We have devoted special attention to quantum computing in this book. It is truly the future of technology. However, the «tech media» does not focus on it as much as it should, which made it necessary for us to enlighten the reader about its importance and its potential impact on the future of organizations.

كان ملؤ عقلي صورتك وأنت فرحة بكتاب حفيدتك
فأحكي لك عن كل تفصيلة عن كل لحظة جهد وتعب
حتى أسمع دعائك لي ولها وكأني طفلة جاءت
لتأخذ جائزتها ... فصبرًا حتى تحين لقياك

9 789948 192015

www.ingramcontent.com/pod-product-compliance
Ingram Content Group UK Ltd.
Pitfield, Milton Keynes, MK11 3LW, UK
UKHW060102300726
14090UKWH00003B/357

* 9 7 8 9 9 4 8 1 9 2 0 1 5 *